OPENING CRED

CW00497922

Contributors this issue: James Aaron, Simon J. Ballard, Rachel Bellwoar, David Michael Brown, Jonathon Dabell, David Flack, Brian Gregory, John Harrison, Bryan C. Kuriawa, James Lecky, Tom Lisanti, Stephen Mosley, Kevin Nickelson, Allen Rubinstein, Peter Sawford, Ian Talbot Taylor, Dr Andrew C. Webber., Steven West. Caricature artwork by Aaron Stielstra.

All articles, photographs and specially produced artwork remain copyright their respective author/photographer/artist. Opinions expressed herein are those of the individual.

Design and Layout: Dawn Dabell
Copy Editor: Jonathon Dabell

Most images in this magazine come from the private collection of Dawn and Jonathon Dabell, or the writer of the corresponding article. Those which do not are made available in an effort to advance understanding of cultural issues pertaining to academic research. We believe this constitutes 'fair use' of any such copyrighted material as provided for in Section 107 of the US Copyright Law. In accordance with Title U.S.C Section 107, this magazine is sold to those who have expressed a prior interest in receiving the included information for research, academic and educational purposes.

Printed globally by Amazon KDP

Editing Room

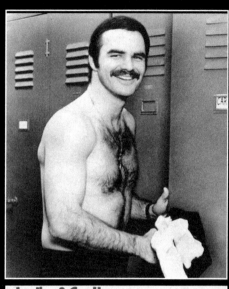

Greetings once more, '70s movie lovers!

After what seems like a long hiatus since Issue 9, we're delighted to be back with Issue 10 of this print-on-demand magazine celebrating the films and film stars of the 1970s.

The grim reaper has certainly been busy since the previous mag, removing some major names from the mortal coil - the likes of Glenda Jackson, William Friedkin, Ryan O'Neal, Richard Roundtree and Alan Arkin to name a few. We should always be thankful we have their wonderful film work to enjoy and remember them by once they are no longer with us.

On a less morbid note, we're really excited by the smorgasbord of fascinating content we're offering in the latest edition. David Michael Brown's cover article about the '70s films of Burt Reynolds is, we feel, a particularly good read and will hopefully inspire you to go out and discover some of Burt's forgotten entries as well as revisiting old favourites. Other articles focus on such eclectic fare as the decade's rock 'n' roll movies, *Moonraker*, *Silver Bears*, *The Warriors*, *Lisa and the Devil*, *The Duellists* and much, much more.

Reaching our tenth issue is something of a milestone. When we launched this magazine in 2020 at the height of the Covid pandemic, we had no idea if there would be an audience for it nor if it would be well enough received to last beyond that inaugural edition. Yet here we are, three and a bit years down the line, offering the tenth magazine (with the fifth issue of the sister publication 'Cinema of the '80s' due out imminently too). We owe the success we've enjoyed so far to our lovely writing family, an assortment of professional scribes and enthusiastic amateurs, and to you - our dear readers - who keep returning for more, offering the sort of praise and encouragement which motivates us to carry on.

Enjoy Issue 10, and we hope to see you again when #11 comes out.

Dawn and Jonathon Dabell.

Remembering Ryan O'Neal (1941-2023)

On December 8th, 2023, Ryan O'Neal died at the age of 82. For the last twenty years of his life, he had been battling several health issues, including leukaemia, prostate cancer and heart disease. His cause of death was listed as congestive heart failure with cardiomyopathy as a contributing factor.

After training as an amateur boxer in his youth, O'Neal took up acting in the '60s, and reached the peak of his stardom in the '70s. He was sometimes criticised for lacking emotional range, but despite this he appeared in some of the decade's most critically and commercially successful films. His '70s output was:

The Games (1970)
Love Story (1970)
Love Hate Love (1971) (TV movie)
What's Up, Doc? (1972)
The Thief Who Came to Dinner (1973)
Paper Moon (1973)
Barry Lyndon (1975)
Nickelodeon (1976)
A Bridge Too Far (1977)
The Driver (1978)
Oliver's Story (1978)
The Main Event (1979)

Farewell, Mr O'Neal. Thanks for the memories.

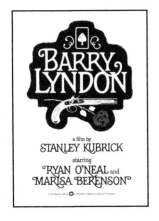

In Memoriam

**Joss Ackland
(1928-2023)**
Actor, known for *Royal Flash* (1975) and *Silver Bears* (1977).

**Alan Arkin
(1934-2023)**
Actor, known for *Catch-22* (1970) and *Freebie and the Bean* (1974).

**Jane Birkin
(1946-2023)**
Actress, known for *Romance of a Horsethief* (1971) and *Death on the Nile* (1978).

**William Friedkin
(1935-2023)**
Director, known for *The French Connection* (1971) and *The Exorcist* (1973).

**Gayle Hunnicutt
(1943-2023)**
Actress, known for *Scorpio* (1973) and *The Legend of Hell House* (1973).

**Glenda Jackson
(1936-2023)**
Actress, known for *A Touch of Class* (1973) and *The Romantic Englishwoman* (1975).

**Piper Laurie
(1940-2023)**
Actress, known for *Carrie* (1976) and *Tim* (1979).

**David McCallum
(1933-2023)**
Actor, known for *Frankenstein: The True Story* (1973) and *Dogs* (1976).

**Richard Roundtree
(1942-2023)**
Actor, known for *Shaft* (1971) and *Earthquake* (1974).

**Burt Young
(1940-2023)**
Actor, known for *Rocky* (1976) and *Convoy* (1978).

3 DAYS OF THE CONDOR

"Someone is always willing to pay"

by James Aaron

No other subgenre of American film is more identified with the decade of the '70s than the conspiracy thriller. The movement came about during years of political and social turmoil that culminated with the simultaneous failure of both the Vietnam War and the scandal-ridden presidency of Richard Nixon. Some of the most noteworthy were Alan Pakula's *The Parallax View* (1974) and *All the President's Men* (1976), Francis Ford Coppola's *The Conversation* (1974) and John Schlesinger's *Marathon Man* (1976).

They generally tread on sinister ground: an unwitting everyman is drawn into nefarious plots puppeteered from the governmental shadows by old white men seated around long conference tables. Often the villains sound downright European, as though an American audience might more readily accept a conspiracy of the Other if that "other" speaks with the formal accent of a John Houseman or a Max von Sydow, or is an out and out Nazi as portrayed by Laurence Olivier. The films were equal parts cynical and fatalist, brimming with paranoia and lethal assassins, and they struck a chord with weary filmgoers who had come to suspect their political leaders were more interested in acting in their own best interests than the best interests of the populace they represented.

Among the best of the bunch was *Three Days of the Condor*, released in 1975 and starring one Hollywood heavyweight (Robert Redford) under the assured direction of another (Sydney Pollack). It featured many of the tropes that fans knew well. The nondescript hero, played by Redford. The accented adversary in the form of the aforementioned

Max von Sydow, who literally speaks the world-weary line "I prefer Europe" during the film's climax. The corrupt face of government, embodied by Cliff Robertson. And, most importantly, the cabal of old white men around the prerequisite conference table. Throw in a dash of romance and enough violence and suspense to satisfy the hungriest audience, and *Three Days of the Condor* fits right in with its conspiratorial brethren, while also managing a few new kinks in the end.

The story starts at breakneck speed. The opening remains to this day probably the most well-known sequence in the movie. Joe Turner (Redford) works for the CIA in downtown New York City, though not in any field or operative capacity. *Condor* goes to great pains to establish its protagonist as unheroic. This is nowhere near James Bond stuff; on the contrary, Joe Turner is a ho-hum analyst in the literary analysis section of the company. He and his colleagues pore over writings from all over the world to detect potential hidden messages, patterns, or anything that might provide intelligence value. "I am not a spy. I just read books," he explains later in the story. "We read everything that's published in the world and we feed the plots - dirty tricks, codes - into a computer, and the computer checks against actual CIA plans and operations. I look for leaks, I look for ideas… we read adventures and novels and journals." This is Redford, the '70s golden boy of Hollywood, knowingly playing against type as nebbish bookworm.

After brief character introductions of Turner and his CIA colleagues, set to the mundane hum of electric printers, all hell breaks loose in a shocking scene of cold-blooded violence. Moments after Turner (the titular "Condor" is his CIA codename) steps out of the office to grab lunch, a group of armed men enter the building and abruptly execute all of Turner's colleagues, from the receptionist to the veteran supervisor seemingly in charge of the office operations. Among the murdered is Turner's girlfriend. "I won't scream," she quietly pleads with the assailants, before they gun her down.

When Turner returns to find the normally secure front door inexplicably ajar, he doesn't immediately sense anything amiss as he steps inside the quiet entranceway. That changes when he finds the receptionist shot to death on the floor behind her desk; from there, he proceeds to locate the rest of the victims around the office. Quickly, reality dawns: he could likely be next on the list if the killers find him. Unsure of whom he can trust, Condor goes on the run, and *Three Days of the Condor* becomes a game of intrigue as the protagonist tries to evade his pursuers and uncover the reason behind the attack on his office, all while navigating the blurred lines between friend and foe.

Three Days of the Condor was based on the novel 'Six Days of the Condor' by James Grady. Besides shrinking the timeline, the film changes much about the source material - most notably moving the action from Washington, D.C.

to New York, and changing the conspirators' motives from the more mundane drug trafficking to one of the '70s great societal bad guys, the oil trade. While the movie was conceived after the 1973 Arab oil embargo, the idea to involve the oil industry came just before the infamous waiting lines at the gas pumps plagued consumers. "We were prescient on this picture by accident, not by design," said director Pollack in a 2007 interview with 'Box Office Mojo'. "I wasn't interested in heroin. It was boring. I was interested in something much more complex... I'm much more interested in the CIA guys who are trying to help us and do something immoral than I am about the guys who are just immoral because they want to sell dope and make money."

Already established as one of the decade's Hollywood heavyweights after *The Yakuza* (1974), *The Way We Were* (1973), and *Jeremiah Johnson* (1972) - the latter two of which also starred Redford - Pollack piles on the tension and atmosphere through *Condor*, and deftly balances the louder sequences with quieter moments of character development that allows the dense plot to unfold in a way that is understandable but doesn't give away too much too soon. He also uses the urban jungle of New York to great effect, as Turner makes his way through a maze of dark alleyways and foreboding buildings in a physical representation of the byzantine plot that he navigates at the same time.

All told, Pollack juggles the complicated plot with just enough explanation to balance out the action and not make the movie feel too weighted in either direction. Too little action could make the story seem boring, but too much might render it unintelligible. Fortunately, neither happens here. If there is one misstep, it comes when Kathy Hale (Faye Dunaway) enters the story, an innocent bystander who is basically kidnapped by Turner to use as a shield and provide him a safe hiding place beneath the radar in her apartment. While the plot turn might make some logistical sense, it strains credulity when the pair quickly falls for each other, pausing for a roll through the sack amidst all the sinister goings-on. (Yes, that's an image from the scene front and center on the movie's original poster. Sex sells. I get it.)

Despite that questionable moment, Redford manages to steady things on screen, lending his calming and believable presence to nearly every scene. At that point, Redford was unquestionably one of cinema's brightest stars. In addition to his work with Pollack, he'd gained prominence with starring turns throughout the late '60s and early '70s in crowd-pleasing cultural touchstones like *Butch Cassidy and the Sundance Kid*, *The Sting* and *The Great Gatsby* His familiar face and onscreen personality allowed filmgoers immediate empathy with his character (such is the giant benefit of casting one of the world's most recognizable faces in your movie as a supposed 'everyman'). Audiences knew him and knew him well.

Yet, like any good leading man, Redford imbues Turner with just enough of the ol' Redford magic to make him clearly the good guy even during some of the more troublesome interactions with Dunaway's Kathy. He might have kidnapped her, might have tied her to the bedframe so she couldn't get away, but dammit, he's trying to save the world. Or his own ass, at least.

At the other end of the spectrum is Joubert, the cold and methodical assassin played by Max Von Sydow. Where Redford lends Joe Turner a sense of classic good-guy righteousness, Joubert follows the way of the hired gun, remaining true to the highest bidder while also maintaining a sense of nobility about the darkest aspects of his chosen profession. He is not there to judge - he is there simply to perform the task that he's been paid to perform, with ruthless efficiency.

Throughout the movie, Joubert is tasked with eliminating those who know too much about a conspiracy rooted within the CIA itself, one involving the seizure of Middle Eastern oil fields. As it turns out, the plan had been discovered by the analysts in Joe's office, thus

spurring the wipeout that opens the movie. However, as the film progresses, it becomes evident that Joubert isn't a straightforward antagonist. He develops a form of professional respect for Turner, particularly impressed by how an untrained analyst manages to evade capture and even combat the threats against him.

By the end of the film, the dynamics between Turner and Joubert gradually shift from hunter and prey to wary admirers of each other. During their showdown at the home of one of the CIA's higher-ups, as the full plot is revealed, Joubert provides Turner with insights into the nature of the intelligence world, a realm where loyalties can be fluid, and survival often depends on seeing the wider view and understanding one's role in it rather than adhering to an unyielding moral code. "I don't interest myself in *why*," Joudert tells Turner. "I think more often in terms of *when*, sometimes *where*, always *how much*." As he explains, Joudert has no belief in either side, or any side. "There is no cause. There is only yourself. The belief is in your own precision."

Played to understated perfection by the masterful, commanding von Sydow - one of global cinema's greatest actors over a decorated career that spanned seventy years - Joubert is *Condor*'s true standout, straddling the line between icy villain and pragmatic mercenary. He operates in shades of gray. His calm demeanor, coupled with moments of sharp insight, adds layers to a character

that could have easily been a one-dimensional assassin in the hands of a less capable actor.

Three Days of the Condor was generally well-received when it was unleashed upon theaters in September 1975. Critics appreciated its tight pacing, compelling narrative, and particularly strong performances from Redford and von Sydow. Roger Ebert called it "a well-made thriller, tense and involving." Vincent Canby in the 'New York Times' said *Condor* was a "fast, vivid espionage-betrayal thriller." The film drew praise for its suspenseful atmosphere and the way it combined elements of traditional spy thrillers with contemporary political headlines, and while it did have its detractors, it was largely seen as a successful and engaging thriller that tapped into the zeitgeist of its era. It was a solid hit, with audiences making it the #6 movie at the box office for the year that otherwise belonged to *Jaws*.

Over the years, *Three Days of the Condor* has seen its reputation grow even further. It's often cited as one of the best conspiracy thrillers of the decade that *defined* the conspiracy thriller. It remains a potent window into turbulent times, and a prime example of '70s filmmaking

BURT REYNOLDS IN THE '70s

by David Michael Brown

Burt Reynolds was the '70s. No other actor encapsulated the era so perfectly. The moustache. The rugged good looks. The knowing smirk. The wisecracking charms. All formed part of his winning persona. From 1978 to 1982, he was the world's number one box-office star for five consecutive years, a record he shares with Bing Crosby. A tough guy who wasn't afraid to poke fun at himself, his big breakthrough was *Deliverance* in 1972 but it could have been different. The *Smokey and the Bandit* (1977) star was also considered for the role of Sonny Corleone in *The Godfather* (1972) before Francis Ford Coppola cast James Caan in the part. And then there was the Brando-Reynolds feud. Reynolds said he couldn't understand Brando's hostility towards him. In a 2015 interview with 'The Guardian', Reynolds said: "He was a strange man. He didn't like me at all." A point proven when he finally met the *Apocalypse Now* (1979) actor. Reynolds said he told him that he was the finest actor in the world. Brando's snide retort was: "I wish I could say the same for you." Reynolds had the last laugh, however, when he finally landed his next role, and gave a performance that would launch his career and elevate him above the television movies and cinematic oddities, like the missing-link adventure *Skullduggery* (1970), that had coloured his career to that point. All it took was a canoe ride.

"I bet you can squeal like a pig!"

When British director John Boorman needed a tough guy as the perfect counterpoint to Jon Voight's city slicker, Ned Beatty's oafish charm and Ronny Cox's guitar-picking businessman, who better to cast than Burt Reynolds playing experienced outdoorsman Lewis? "It's the first time I haven't had a script with Paul Newman's and Robert Redford's fingerprints all over it," Reynolds joked to the 'Chicago Tribune'. "The producers actually came to me first."

His performance as Lewis in the eco-thriller *Deliverance* (1972) is a brilliant exercise in restrained machismo cool. Renowned for its 'Duelling Banjos' soundtrack and the squirm-inducing "He got a real purty mouth, ain't he?" scene, *Deliverance* follows four city-dwelling friends who decide to get away from their jobs, wives and kids for a week of canoeing in rural Georgia on the Cahulawassee River before it is dammed and lost forever. Lewis describes "the vanishing wilderness" as he explains that they're taking a trip down the river before industrialists swoop in and destroy another section of the natural world. "They're drownin' a river, man!"

When the men arrive, they are not welcomed with open arms by the backwards locals who treat them with suspicion, even when trading banjo licks. Ed (Voight) and Bobby (Beatty) are captured, torture and abused, inspiring a whole generation of Hillbilly horror films in the process. Harrowing in the extreme, the shocking scene as the rednecks wail against progress and civilisation is brutal and confronting until Lewis kills one of them with a bow and arrow. It's his moment of heroism before he is incapacitated on the rapids when he breaks his leg.

Reeling from the attack, the men frantically head downriver only to be faced by dangerous rapids and a

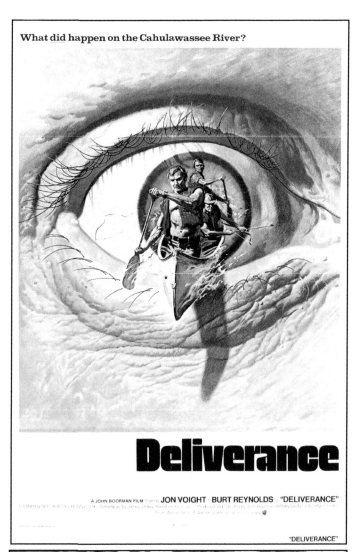

What **did** happen on the Cahulawassee River?

Deliverance

A JOHN BOORMAN FILM starring JON VOIGHT · BURT REYNOLDS in "DELIVERANCE"

"DELIVERANCE"

gun-toting local. For the scene where Lewis dives over the waterfall, Reynolds volunteered to do it for real, as he told 'The Hollywood Reporter': "They let the water go and I heard this sound - I dream sometimes of the water coming - I looked around and there was a tidal wave coming at me. I went over the falls and the first thing that happened I hit a rock and cracked my tailbone, and to this day it hurts. Then I went down to the water below and it was a whirlpool. I couldn't get out and guy there said if you get caught, just go to the bottom. You can get out, but you can't swim against it. So, I went down to the bottom. What he didn't tell me was it was going to shoot me up like a torpedo. So, I went out."

The centrifugal force of the whirlpool separated Reynolds from his costume as he continued: "They said later that they saw this 30-year-old guy in costume go over the waterfall and then about fifteen minutes later they saw this nude man come out. It had torn everything - my boots and everything off."

"Proceed with erection - all systems go".

1972 was a big year for Reynolds. Not only did he head downstream in *Deliverance*, but he posed nude for a 'Cosmo' centrefold, one of his hands strategically covering

HERE COME THE **"FUZZ"**

FILMWAYS presents A MARTIN RANSOHOFF Production
starring
"FUZZ"
BURT REYNOLDS **JACK WESTON** **TOM SKERRITT**
also starring **YUL BRYNNER** as 'The Deaf Man'
and **RAQUEL WELCH**
Executive Producer EDWARD S. FELDMAN Screenplay by EVAN HUNTER
Based on the Novel by ED McBAIN Produced by JACK FARREN Directed by RICHARD A. COLLA
PG PARENTAL GUIDANCE SUGGESTED Music by DAVE GRUSIN A FILMWAYS-JAVELIN Picture **United Artists**

his private parts, and he cameoed in Woody Allen's *Everything You Always Wanted to Know About Sex * But Were Afraid to Ask*. Reynolds is hilarious as a switchboard operator in charge of a man's sperm. He barks orders like, "Proceed with erection - all systems go" and "Erection is at 45 degrees and holding fast" at his body function running underlings. 1972 was also the year that he starred opposite Raquel Welch in *Fuzz*.

Welch did not like Reynolds. Her hatred stemmed from comments he made while they were filming *100 Rifles* (1969) that she considered unsavoury. She insisted that she not have any direct scenes with Reynolds in the film. Adapted from the satirical 87th Precinct Mysteries by Ed McBain, *Fuzz* is a ramshackle police thriller directed by Richard A. Colla after Brian De Palma dropped out over casting disagreements. Set in Boston, the messy deadpan thriller follows detectives Steve Carella (Reynolds), Meyer Meyer (Jack Weston), Bert Kling (Tom Skerritt) and Eileen McHenry (Welch) in hot pursuit of a crime lord known only as the Deaf Man (Yul Brynner) who is on an explosive killing spree bombing local politicians. While tracking down the enigmatic bomber, they must also protect derelicts on the streets who are being set on fire by a group of delinquent teens. When going undercover, Carella is set alight by the hoodlums and desperately tries to take off his burning trench coat. Reynolds almost suffered serious burns to his face while doing the stunt, as out of control flames whipped up his asbestos lined coat sleeve, around his neck, and along the back of his head. This was the cut that made it into the movie.

NYPD estimated three thousand onlookers, mainly women and teenagers, attended the first day of principal photography of *Shamus* (1973) in Brooklyn, New York City. Reynolds plays the titular New York City private investigator Shamus McCoy. The hard-living heel is hired by jewellery baron E.J. Hume (Ron Weyand) to track down a shipment of uncut diamonds. Lured by the lucrative deal, soon Shamus is embroiled with a gun-smuggling ring, an ex-football player named Felix Montaigne (Alex Wilson)

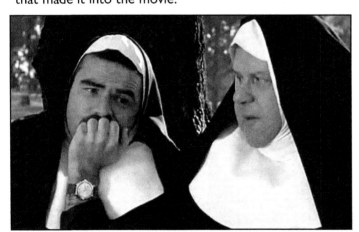

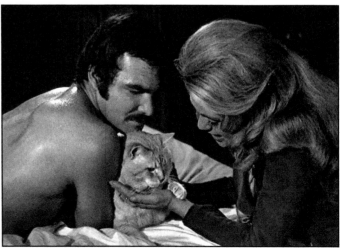

11

and Felix's irresistible sister, Alexis (Dyan Cannon). Set in a gritty New York City and playing like a Chandler-esque noir with sexist cops, *Shamus* is a hard-boiled thriller with a muscular edge as Reynolds strangles one poor soul with a chain wrapped around their neck, with a sadistic look of glee on his face.

Reynolds wrote about his co-star Cannon in his autobiography 'My Life' (1994): "As Dyan and I walked down Broadway one afternoon a guy stopped us and asked for a picture. A camera dangled around his neck. 'Well, okay,' I said. Grinning broadly, he put his arm around Dyan and handed me the camera."

The western *The Man Who Loved Cat Dancing* (1973) followed and saw a dishevelled unshaven Reynolds returning to the western genre playing Jay Grobart, a crest-fallen man out for vengeance after his native American wife Cat Dancing is murdered. Juggling train robbery with single parenting, Jay reluctantly turns to a life of crime. When his accomplices kidnap society woman Catherine Crocker (Sarah Miles), Grobart's moral compass forces him to protects her as they flee from the bounty hunter (Lee J. Cobb) and her violent husband (George Hamilton).

Directed by Richard C. Sarafian and based on the novel written by Marilyn Durham first published in 1972, the film was not an enormous success. Even Reynold said: "it's not as good as the book."

"I was born ready!"

Then came the first appearance of Georgia moonshiner and ex-convict Gator McKlusky in *White Lightning* (1973). When we join him, the smooth-talking Arkansas good ol' boy is serving his second federal prison sentence for running moonshine. When his clean-cut college graduate brother and his girlfriend are brutally murdered, Gator suspects that corrupt county sheriff J.C. Connors (Ned Beatty) is responsible. The jailbird makes a deal with the federal attorney to get out of prison so he can infiltrate Connors' illicit booze-running operation. Hugely entertaining, the southern fried actioner was the film that created the template for Reynolds the movie star. From fast cars, bad cops, frisky women, dodgy sexism and good old-fashioned brawn.

White Lightning also highlighted one of Hollywood's most dangerous double acts. Macho hellraisers Reynolds and his body-double stuntman Hal Needham were the inspiration behind Rick Dalton (Leonardo DiCaprio)

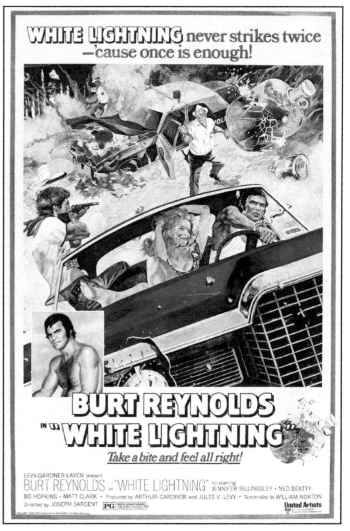

and his stunt double sidekick Cliff Booth (Brad Pitt) in Quentin Tarantino's *Once Upon a Time... in Hollywood* (2019). Needham lived with Reynolds for 12 years in his outhouse. He began to double for Burt in the early '60s on the TV series *Riverboat* and the pair would go on to work together in classics like *Gator, The Cannonball Run,* the first two *Smokey and the Bandit* films and *Hooper.* The famous stunt scene in *White Lightning,* where McKlusky drives off a pier onto a barge, barely hitting it, actually was a real on-screen accident. They misjudged the speed of the barge and the car ended up being destroyed, almost killing Needham. Reynolds dove into the water and helped pull his friend to safety. Reynolds told AOL, "I thought he was - and he was - the best stuntman that ever lived."

As an interesting footnote, Steven Spielberg almost directed the film. "I spent two-and-a-half months on the film, met Burt once, found most of the locations and began to cast the movie until I realized it wasn't something that I wanted to do for a first film. I didn't want to start my career as a hard-hat, journeyman director. I wanted to do something that was a little more personal."

"Couldn't find a car wash."

Robert Aldrich's *The Longest Yard* (1974) - known as *The Mean Machine* in the UK - was the first collaboration between Reynolds and *The Godfather* producer Albert S. Ruddy. The gritty sporting comedy saw Reynolds play Paul 'Wrecking' Crewe, a former pro quarterback now serving time in prison after taking his ex-girlfriend's Maserati-engined Citroën SM for a drunken spin without permission

and leading police on a wild car chase. The sadistic Warden Hazen (Eddie Albert) forces the ex-gridiron player to organise a team of inmates, who become known as the Mean Machine, to take on the guards. Hazen tries to blackmail Crewe into throwing the game in exchange for an early release but the convicts, tired of taking a good kicking from the prison staff, want to dish out some vengeful brutality of their own on the pitch.

He followed *The Longest Yard* with the country music comedy *W.W. and the Dixie Dancekings* (1975) and then co-starred with *Taxi Driver*'s Cybill Shepherd in Peter

Bogdanovich's musical rom-com *At Long Last Love* (1975). Then he returned to type with Aldrich again on the jaded, cynical, edgy cop thriller *Hustle* (1975). He played Lt. Phil Gaines, another tough-talking detective, this time based in Los Angeles, who is investigating the apparent suicide of a teenage girl who he discovers was a stripper and a prostitute. Complicating matters is his relationship with a hooker, played by French actress Catherine Deneuve, whose high-powered client, powerful mob lawyer Leo Sellers (Eddie Albert), is a person of interest for the police.

Reynolds said of his co-star while talking to noted film critic Roger Ebert: "The nice thing about working with Deneuve was that she'd only seen one of my films, the best one, *Deliverance*. She didn't know about all the Burt Reynolds B.S. over here. I went to Paris and talked her into making *Hustle* because she thought I was funny. I laughed her into it."

Gene Hackman and Liza Minnelli joined Reynolds for Stanley Donen's *Lucky Lady* (1975) about a trio of rum-runners during prohibition in the '30s who engage in a steamy menage-a-trois after business hours. "I loved Liza Minnelli and Gene Hackman, and I loved the Jack Lemmon kind of character I played," Reynolds said of the poorly received film. "But there were times when I felt Stanley Donen was petrified and lost. Scared of the boats, scared of the explosions, of the gunshots. I'd look at him between takes and he'd be like this [crouching with hands over his head]. But the bedroom scene with the three of us was so beautifully done. I remember going to rushes and saying, 'This is going to be a winner - it really works.' It was a beautifully mounted picture, but the last forty minutes, the battle, was not his kind of film. Nobody knew what was happening and you didn't care for the characters."

"Why they call you Bones?"

Interestingly, George Lucas and Gary Kurtz used the film as a crew storefront and hiring many of the predominantly British filmmakers while making *Star Wars*, a film that Reynolds was also offered when Lucas wanted him to play Han Solo. Reynolds declined, as he did for the role of James Bond. After a hilarious cameo in *Silent Movie* (1976) that saw Reynolds playing a vain version of himself sharing a sudsy shower with Mel Brooks, Dom DeLuise and Marty Feldman, he directed his first feature, returning to the character of Gator

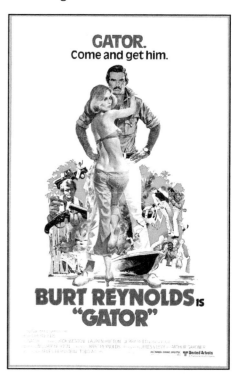

McKlusky for *Gator* (1976).

"I play a former moonshiner who's an FBI type," he explained to Roger Ebert, "and I get into this relationship with a girl, played by Lauren Hutton. I'm a guy who thinks a Martini is an Italian boxer, and she's a very modern lady who wants to be Barbara Walters. We make love, and I, being a male chauvinist pig, think that means a commitment." *Gator* certainly continues where White Lightning left off with a huge high-speed boat chase in the Everglades as the notorious ex-con and moonshine distiller moves in with his father in a cabin in the Okefenokee Swamp after he is released from prison. Returning to his bootlegging ways, a federal agent tells McKlusky that he will lose custody of his 9-year-old daughter unless he helps bring down a local crime lord and former boyhood pal Bama McCall (played by Jerry Reed who would go on to be a Reynolds regular). Gator is torn, not wanting to go against his old friend until he discovers that Bama is involved in corruption, murder and is prostituting spaced-out under-age cheerleaders.

After his experience directing himself, he stepped in front of the camera for Bogdanovich's breezy comedy *Nickelodeon* (1976). Bogdanovich co-wrote the problematic love letter to Hollywood's pioneering years with W.D. Richter, the writer of Philip Kaufman's excellent *Invasion of the Body Snatchers* (1979) remake and director of *The Adventures of Buckaroo Banzai Across the 8th Dimension* (1984). Set in the silent film era before 1915's *Birth of a Nation* changed the face of cinema, Bogdanovich regular Ryan O'Neal plays attorney Leo Harrigan and Reynolds takes on the role of rugged gunslinger Buck Greenway. The pair are hired to put stop to an illegal film production

but instead, inadvertently team up with the filmmakers. Leo becomes a director, and Buck an inexplicable leading man. But soon movies are the last thing on their minds when the pair find themselves waging war over the heart of beautiful starlet Kathleen Cooke (Jane Hitchcock).

"For the money, for the glory, and for the fun... mostly for the money."

Then came the film that saw Reynolds become a global megastar. Directed by Hal Needham, *Smokey and the Bandit* was the ultimate Burt Reynolds movie. He played the boisterous bootlegger hired by wealthy Texan Big Enos Burdette (Pat McCormick) and his son Little Enos (Paul Williams) to run an articulated truck illegally loaded with 400 cases of Coors beer over state lines. With redneck sheriff (Jackie Gleason) on their tail, Bandit recklessly drives his Trans Am with a runaway bride (Sally Field starting an on-screen and off-screen relationship with Reynolds) riding shotgun while Cledus (Jerry Reed) sits behind the wheel of the artic. A non-stop car chase from Texarkana to Atlanta, *Smokey and the Bandit* runs on Reynold's charm offensive as much as petrol.

IT'S THE WORLD'S GREATEST GAME
(AND IT SURE AIN'T FOOTBALL.)

starring
DAVID MERRICK presents A MICHAEL RITCHIE Film
BURT REYNOLDS · KRIS KRISTOFFERSON
JILL CLAYBURGH
"SEMI-TOUGH"
ROBERT PRESTON as 'Big Ed Bookman' Screenplay by WALTER BERNSTEIN
Based upon a novel by DAN JENKINS Produced by DAVID MERRICK Directed by MICHAEL RITCHIE
United Artists

"I think they were the one and the same!" laughed *Phantom of the Paradise* (1974) star Williams when asked about his charismatic co-star. "It was the easiest acting job in the world for him, you know. There was a certain level of comfort for him on *Smokey*. First of all, Hal Needham was just fantastic, and they were tight buddies. They were always in the football huddle together on set, and I often wondered what actually was being shared in those huddles. Were they talking about the next shot or was it more like, 'What are you doing later?'"

Second only to *Star Wars* at the box-office in 1977, the raucous road movie spawned two sequels and cemented Reynolds' public persona as a loveable good ol' boy who had an eye for the ladies, a beer for his buddies and nothing but disdain for the authorities. It was a persona he created with Gator and would continue with Hooper, but Bandit was the character that audiences flocked to see. "The film I had the most fun on was *Smokey and the Bandit*," the actor said during a 2015 interview at the Macon Film Festival. "And I still have one of the Trans Ams from the film."

In 1977, Reynolds returned to the American football pitch in *Semi-Tough* (1977) alongside Kris Kristofferson. Reynolds plays Billy Clyde Puckett, a professional American footballer who shares a lush Miami apartment with Marvin 'Shake' Tiller (Kristofferson) and Barbara Jane (Jill Clayburgh), the daughter of the Miami club's owner. All is well on and of the pitch until Barbara and Shake start a relationship, causing a rift between the two friends. With Reynolds wearing the uniform number 22, just as he did in *The Longest Yard* (1974), the actor along with Kristofferson was training with professional athletes to get themselves into shape. Kristofferson broke a couple

of bones for his efforts.

"I've got a date with a 38."

After briefly working together for Mel Brooks on *Silent Movie*, Reynolds and Dom DeLuise teamed up for the pitch-black comedy *The End* (1978). Reynolds directed and headlined as Wendell 'Sonny' Lawson, an unscrupulous real-estate promoter who learns he has a fatal blood disease and has only a year to live. After trying to settle things with his ex-wife (Sally Field), he decides to kill himself quickly rather than endure a slow, undignified death. He tries to find a way of doing himself in without hurting himself and ends up in a mental institution, where he befriends a fellow patient, Marlon Borunki (DeLuise), a deranged schizophrenic who is keen to help him succeed.

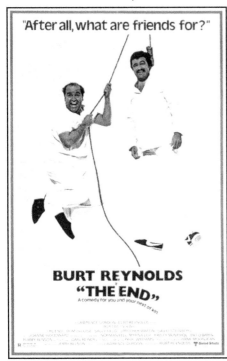

Full of pratfalls, overacting, bad taste gags and the always wonderful Field, the potentially suicidal career move worked wonders with audiences and once again proved Reynolds box-office mettle.

Reynolds said of his beloved co-star DeLuise during a Q&A at a screening of *The Cannonball Run* at Hollywood Palms Cinema in 2011: "I've never had anyone make me laugh so much - anytime, anywhere, anyplace. The strange thing was I could make him laugh anytime, anyplace, anywhere, which became kind of a catastrophe when we were trying to get a shot done. Because when he had the giggles, I had the giggles."

Reynolds and DeLuise obviously enjoyed working together and collaborated again on *Smokey and the Bandit Ride Again* (1980), *The Cannonball Run* (1981), *The Best Little Whorehouse in Texas* (1982) and *Cannonball Run II* (1984).

Reynolds may have made his last film of the decade in the company of Jill Clayburgh and Candice Bergen in Alan J. Pakula's *Starting Over* (1979), playing a divorced man who is torn between his new girlfriend and his ex-wife, but it was *Hooper* (1978) that played like a "Burt Reynolds Greatest Hits of the '70s". Reuniting him with Needham and Field a year after *Smokey and the Bandit*, the

THE GREATEST STUNTMAN ALIVE!

filmmaking comedy paid tribute to the men and women who risked their lives every day in the name of Hollywood Reynolds plays Tinsel Town's top stuntman Sonny Hooper. He is hired as the stunt coordinator for big-budget action movie *The Spy Who Laughed at Danger* complete with a pushy director (Robert Klein) and a hapless lead (Adam West). Feeling his age and worried about his own mortality, Hooper decides to make the film's climactic stunt in a rocket car his biggest ever, while young upstart Delmore 'Ski' Shidski (Jan-Michael Vincent) tries to prove that modern technology is taking over from good old-fashioned grit. The practical stunts are astounding but looking past the high-octane thrills and this is a paean to a golden era of filmmaking. Reynolds perfectly mixes his cocksure personality with a surprisingly intimate moment of personal realisation when he strips down to his briefs to look over his battle-scarred body. Even the indestructible Reynolds is human.

The Undecided Spaghetti Western

by Tom Lisanti

"LOS AMIGOS"

In 1973, the Paolo Cavara-directed, Joseph Janni-produced western *Los Amigos* (translation: *The Friends*) opened worldwide. In some English-speaking territories it went by the title *Deaf Smith and Johnny Ears*. Set during a time of upheaval in Texas, the film stars Anthony Quinn as a deaf and mute mercenary named Eratus 'Deaf' Smith (who was a real-life hearing-impaired scout, although not mute, for Sam Houston, the president of the Republic of Texas) and Franco Nero as is his woman-crazy partner Johnny Ears (a totally fictional character). When an ex-general attempts to install himself as dictator of a newly independent Texas, Sam calls in Deaf Smith for help. The film also features Pamela Tiffin in one of her best roles as an angelic-faced, feisty whore with a heart of gold who falls in love with Johnny.

From the get-go, Cavara made pronouncements that he was not making a spaghetti western. That genre had begun in 1964 with a trio of Sergio Leone-directed violent westerns starring Clint Eastwood as the Man-with-No-Name and peaked during the late '60s. Cavara remarked: "The day of those blood-and-guts oaters made over here is over." He went on to call his movie a 'psychological western' which he also infused with humor. Cavara was adamant about this and made a point of bringing it up whenever he spoke about the film.

The story is credited to American writers Harry Essex and Oscar Paul. They had written it a few years earlier and originally their screenplay was optioned by Sinatra Enterprises as a potential starring feature for Frank Sinatra (who would have played Smith). That version never came to be. They also received sole screenplay credit despite rewrites by Cavara and others.

Cavara began casting the film knowing that he wanted a mature and a young actor for the leads. He explained: "With an older man and a younger man, you have covered all of life. The older man has experience and knows about life; the younger man represents youth and its desire to change everything. Thus conflict."

Nero was very excited to make this western, but he thought he would be playing Deaf Smith. He revealed: "The producer was an Italian named Joseph Janni who used to work in England. He produced some great movies. One day he came to Italy to meet with me and said: 'I would like to do something like *Midnight Cowboy* about two friends. One talks all the time and the other is mute.' I replied: 'I would love to play the one who doesn't talk.' He then told me that Anthony Quinn had already read the script and wanted to play the deaf mute. I said: 'But he is American and is more comfortable speaking English.' We went back and forth for about a month. Getting nowhere,

Janni then set up a meeting with him, me, and Tony. It was very funny. Tony kept insisting he play the part and I kept saying: 'But you are the American!' At the end, we decided to flip a coin. Whoever wins plays Deaf Smith. We did and Tony won."

With the actors finally settled into their roles, Cavara was hopeful that Nero and Quinn would replicate the classic partnering of Montgomery Clift and John Wayne in the western *Red River*.

Janni's next task was to cast the female lead. He knew he would need a beautiful actress who could also be funny, for the role of Susie, the hooker who falls for Johnny. Nero had only one actress in mind for the part. "Pamela Tiffin was cast because of me," he boasted. "We were both very popular. I remember talking to my agent Paola Petri and saying that I would love to have Pamela in the movie because she was born to play comedy." Tiffin became Nero's leading lady for the second time (the first being the giallo *Il giornata nera per l'Ariete* in 1971).

Pamela jumped at the chance to work with Quinn and Nero. The fact that it was a western made it even more attractive to her. She exclaimed: "I love westerns because I love nature and that kind of folklore."

Although Quinn and Nero were big names in westerns, this was only Tiffin's second appearance in the genre since the John Sturges-directed 1965 epic *The Hallelujah Trail*

starring Burt Lancaster. Surprisingly, since she had been living in Rome and working in Italian cinema since 1967, *Los Amigos* was her first western made there despite the large number of spaghetti westerns produced during this period.

Receiving fourth billing, in a small role, was the beautiful Ira von Fürstenberg (billed as Ira Fürstenberg and reportedly stepping in for Marisa Mell) who spends the majority of her screen time with Quinn. Ira was also in *Il giornata nera per l'Ariete* with Nero and Tiffin. Pamela remarked: "I was never in a scene with Ira von Fürstenberg but she is competitive. I remember there was an opening cast party and she wouldn't talk to me."

Los Amigos (budgeted at $1.2 million) was an Italian co-production between companies in Rome and Milan with MGM picking up the international distribution rights. Filming began in October 1972, but not in Spain where most Italian westerns were shot. Instead, the cast and crew headed to Calabria in southern Italy for four weeks before moving to Rome to shoot interiors at Elios Studios.

The week before production was to commence, Cavara took his actors to the desert region near Bari, located on the southern tip of the Italian peninsula. He explained: "I wanted them to bum around a bit and do nothing but absorb. By the time we started shooting I really didn't have to exert myself. I became almost an editor. A good

cast is a director's best insurance outside of his script."

Another thing that Cavara did, which was outside of the norm for Italian filmmaking at the time, was to record direct sound while filming. For most movies, all of the dialog was looped afterwards and added in post-production, along with sound effects. *Il giornata nera per l'Ariete* was also shot with direct sound and that is why Franco and Tiffin's real voices can be heard in the English-language versions of both movies. Italian films were slowly pulling away from looping entire movies in the dubbing booths. Nero remarked: "In Italy, at the time, the mentality was not to shoot direct sound because noise would be picked up and they would dub everything. I remember my character at the beginning in the script was an American. I said: 'I can't play an American. I have an accent.' They re-wrote it to make an excuse for my accent. So, my character states he is Spanish. In westerns, they can always find an excuse not to be pure American."

Cavara picked his crew wisely, especially his cinematographer - the brilliant and prolific Tonino Delli Colli. His prior credits included Sergio Leone's classic westerns *The Good, the Bad and the Ugly* and *Once Upon a Time in the West*. His work on those films is considered to be some of the very best photography in the westerns of the period.

Quinn, who had appeared in numerous westerns prior to *Los Amigos*, desperately wanted the role sof Eratus Smith because he felt it would be a challenge to play a deaf-mute. However, as shooting began, he knew he needed guidance. He commented: "When I started to play the part it was so tricky that I knew I was in danger of overdoing it. I went to Cavara and asked him to hold me down and keep me in line." One of Quinn's favorite directors was Stanley Kramer, who he called "an actor's director." They worked together on the Golden Globe Award-winning WWII comedy *The Secret of Santa Vittoria* (1969) and the less successful campus unrest drama *R.P.M.* (1970). Comparing Cavara to Kramer, Quinn opined: "Cavara doesn't have Kramer's tough attitude, but operates his own way. He is a very sensitive man, a diplomat. He gets what *he* wants. A director must never be afraid of an actor no matter how big he is." Perhaps it was this sensitivity that made Cavara determined not to make *Los Amigos* in the spaghetti western-style and instead to strive for something different.

Though Nero felt that *Los Amigos* was an easy, pleasant shoot, the actor was not as enarmored with the director. "Paola Cavara was very professional," opined Nero. "They gave him the script and he did his job. I would not call him a very creative director. But we got lucky because we had the great cinematographer, Tonino Delli Colli. He was fantastic and had worked with Fellini and Leone."

Filming seemed to have progressed smoothly and everyone got along nicely. Pamela exclaimed, "I so enjoyed making this movie. Anthony Quinn is larger than life and

is attractive in a primordial kind of way. He was very easy to work with. Franco Nero is very tall, very handsome, and very decent. He had the impact in Europe that Paul Newman had in America."

Nero concurred with Pamela and remarked: "Tony, Pamela, and I got along greatly. We had such a fun time making this film." He then added with a mischievous laugh: "I admit if I was not already - how can I say? Engaged? - I would have loved to have - you know - with Pamela. But I never did."

The actor did hold a special place in Pamela's heart because he helped her during a love scene where she needed to perform topless. Per Tiffin: "I said to Franco I didn't want my bosom to show. He understood and we thought how could we outsmart the director? We found a way to hold each other very tight or he'd have an elbow or an arm in the way. I can remember the frustrated director shouting in Italian: 'Do it again!' We'd respond: 'Well, we just did it!' Sometimes actors band together in a wonderful way. I'll always be grateful to him."

Nero remembers this incident and takes no special bows for coming to the aid of a fellow actor. He said:

Metro-Goldwyn-Mayer presents
"DEAF SMITH AND JOHNNY EARS"

MGM Presents
"DEAF SMITH & JOHNNY EARS"
Metrocolor

DEAF SMITH & JOHNNY EARS ... ANTHONY QUINN FRANCO NERO ... PAMELA TIFFIN

DEAF SMITH & JOHNNY EARS ... ANTHONY QUINN FRANCO NERO ... PAMELA TIFFIN

"Pamela was feeling uncomfortable about doing the scene so I helped her. She said, 'Franco, I don't want my bosom to show.' I didn't think the movie was the kind that had to show bosoms anyway. It wasn't called for in this western that was funny and very violent. It really wasn't about sex."

Quinn also liked working on this movie and especially enjoyed playing Deaf Smith. It was a part that helped him grow as an actor since he had to really listen to others, a trait he felt most actors lacked. He remarked: "If every actor could play a deaf-mute once it would be the best thing that could happen to him. I had to react to everything and everyone around me. It was a terrific experience."

Los Amigos opens with Anthony Quinn and Franco Nero roaming the prairie. A voice-over by Nero informs the audience that Quinn's Eratus Smith is a deaf-mute who understands people by reading lips. He is described as a hero and President Houston's personal spy. Nero is his Spanish partner Juanito, nicknamed Johnny Ears. He gets Deaf Smith's attention by throwing stones at him. They have been sent by the president to aid a general in Austin, Texas, who is trying to subvert a group of rebels, backed by a foreign power, from preventing the newly formed

Republic of Texas becoming part of the United States. The pair have various adventures and romances during the course of their mission.

Los Amigos was re-titled *Deaf Smith & Johnny Ears* when released in the U.S. (and the United Kingdom) in the spring of 1973 with the tagline: "The Man who hears with his eyes and speaks with his gun… He lives to kill. And he's gonna live it up tonight."

Despite Cavara's insistence that the movie was not a spaghetti western, due to the fact that Nero's character is more interested in loving than fighting (atypical for a hero in this genre), mainstream reviewers seemed to disagree with him. And most opined that *Deaf Smith & Johnny Ears* was not a very good western, no matter what type it was labeled.

'New York Times' critic A.H. Weiler commented that the movie "is as limp an example of the so-called 'spaghetti western' as has turned up in recent memory" and "an ersatz adventure that is neither as explosive or as funny as most movies in the genre." The reviewer in 'Cue' called it "an exercise in dullness and ineptitude." Rex Reed for the 'New York Daily News' wrote: "There is nothing to commend this paella western." Even 'Variety' had poor words, calling the movie "a mostly dull, occasionally ludicrous oater sorely lacking in the excessive violence or marquee voltage that might earn it an action-loving audience." Alan R. Howard of the 'Hollywood

Reporter' slammed the movie for being "a pedestrian western, long on talk, awkwardly structured and neither as endearing nor comic as it's supposed to be." One good review came from 'The Independent Film Journal' which called it "a slight cut above the spaghetti western." Tiffin was amusingly singled out by its critic who said that she "bounces through her moments with a bit more pizzazz than she showed in Hollywood with the result that the sauce on this spaghetti is not that untasty."

Perhaps the negative reviews the movie received were due to the overload of European westerns that were flooding the screens. On its own, *Deaf Smith & Johnny Ears* is quite entertaining. The premise of the leads being alternately deaf and mute is a novel and intriguing idea. There are some nice touches, like seeing the action through Deaf Smith's eyes with no sound. Though quite amusing for the most part, the plot is a bit implausible expecting moviegoers to believe that the fate of Texas is left in the hands of only two men. It is also full of plot holes. Ira Fürstenberg looks as if she is going to be an important character, but after sneaking Deaf Smith into her house to spy on her husband, she disappears from the movie completely despite her fourth billing.

Even with these minor shortcomings, the movie is highly recommended and buoyed by the three lead actors. Quinn is quite expressive without saying a word. Nero is utterly charming and in fine comedic form as Johnny Ears and has

a good rapport with Quinn. He does his best to bridge the energetic humorous scenes with Tiffin's hooker with the more somber and serious scenes with Quinn's deaf scout. The movie really rests on Nero's shoulders and he succeeds in projecting Johnny's love for Susie alongside his need to be needed by Deaf Smith. However, it is like watching two different movies. This is a western where the interplay between the characters is the most interesting aspect of the film. Usually, it is the reverse with the talky moments getting in the way of the action.

As for Tiffin, she is a vision of loveliness from the moment she first appears on screen bathing in a creek. Nero was correct in recommending her for the part. She perfectly portrays Susie's excitement that quickly turns to anger when she realizes that she is competing with Smith for Johnny's affections. Despite his protestations about how he cannot desert his deaf friend, Susie intuitively realizes that it is actually a weak Johnny who is dependant on Smith, using Smith's disability as an excuse not to leave him.

The film's poor reviews doomed its box office chances. It was not a hit in the U.S. and disappeared from most theaters in a week or less. It couldn't even recoup its modest $1.2 million dollar budget. It was definitely a victim of bad timing and, despite director Cavara's emphatic statements that was a conventional western, audiences in America automatically associated it with the spaghetti western genre which had long since peaked in the U.S. Perhaps if it had been made a few years prior, it would have attracted a larger audience.

Box office-wise it fared no better in Italy, grossing 421,241 lira (roughly $285,364). In comparison, Tonino Valeri's western *My Name Is Nobody* made 3,620,000 lire ($2.5 million) at the box office that same year. Luckily, however, the movie did better business elsewhere especially in the UK. When it opened in London, it was the highest grossing new film that week.

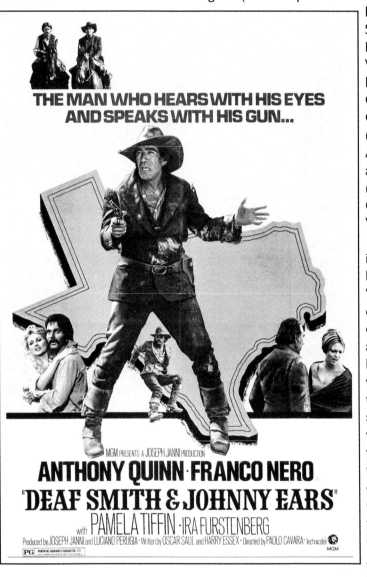

THE MAN WHO HEARS WITH HIS EYES AND SPEAKS WITH HIS GUN...

MGM PRESENTS A JOSEPH JANNI PRODUCTION
ANTHONY QUINN · FRANCO NERO
"DEAF SMITH & JOHNNY EARS"
with PAMELA TIFFIN · IRA FURSTENBERG
Produced by JOSEPH JANNI and LUCIANO PERUGIA · Written by OSCAR SAUL and HARRY ESSEX · Directed by PAOLO CAVARA · Technicolor
PG PARENTAL GUIDANCE SUGGESTED

Today, there is a revisionist view of the movie, and it is considered much more memorable than when first released. And despite Cavara's insistence that it was not a spaghetti western, most film historians and aficionados (Franco Nero as well) consider *Los Amigos* to be part of the spaghetti western genre. The movie is a part of such websites as The Spaghetti Western Database, Shobarry's Spaghetti Westerns, and Fistful of Pasta. The film is also included in books about spaghetti westerns by Howard Hughes ('Once Upon a Time in the Italian West: The Filmgoers' Guide to Spaghetti Westerns', 'The Kamera Guide to Spaghetti Westerns', and 'Cinema Italiano: The Complete Guide from Classics to Cult'); Bert Fridlund ('The Spaghetti Western: A Thematic Analysis') and Thomas Weisser ('Spaghetti Westerns: The Good, the Bad, and the Violent').

Explaining why he included *Los Amigos* in his books, Hughes remarked: "It bears all the hallmarks of the genre: the music, the desert, the showdowns, and the violence. The two heroes take on a renegade who is ruling a town with terror tactics and the finale sees them attacking the villain's stockade fortress, which was a popular ending to European westerns of the period, such as *El Condor*... I'm very fond of this movie and it remains one of the unheralded gems of the Italian western genre."

More recently, film collector Joe Secrett penned an article about the 1977 spaghetti western *Mannaja* starring Maurizio Merli for a prior issue of 'Cinema of the '70s'. He mentions that more light-hearted, "comedy-western hybrids" emerged during the early '70s, which prolonged the life of the spaghetti western genre. *Los Amigos* fits that bill.

Despite Cavara's insistence, he is outnumbered and most film historians consider *Los Amigos* part of the spaghetti western genre (sorry Paolo).

SCUM

by Brian Gregory

As a school kid in the '80s, I could always rely on the older boys in the neighbourhood to show me terrifying films on video. In my primary school years there was Jason Brooker, two years older and just two doors down, who would reliably play me the latest horror flicks, way before I reached the accepted viewing age, often preceded by the latest heavy metal vinyl releases blasting from his stereo (a perfect prelude). While in the next road, during my high school years, the Jones brothers, Gareth and Evan, eagerly introduced me to the uncompromising world of Alan Clarke (via the brutality of *Scum*, the raw football violence of *The Firm* and the cold sectarian executions of *Elephant*). They all left a lasting impression, and, even to this day, Evan and I will effortlessly fall into quoting *Scum*'s standout scenes verbatim when we meet up. In fact, those impressionable teenage years were the perfect time to encounter Clarke's output. You wouldn't show it to your peers but, as you giggled together darkly, his films' searing honesty both fascinated and scared the crap out of you in equal measure, each one haunting your soul long after viewing. These were no easy watches and during those years, thanks to *Scum*, I feared being locked up almost as much as I feared nuclear war. Alan Clarke was about as honest a filmmaker as Britain has ever produced. Supremely talented, he was always totally (here comes that word again) uncompromising in his art and I instinctively respected him for it. Clarke's films were (and still are) the perfect British antidote to glossy Hollywood movies, which seemed alien to my less-than-glossy world of '80s suburban London, my four television channels and my drab, tedious state secondary school. Of course, another reason why teenagers were drawn to them was that Clarke's work defiantly held two fingers up to the establishment.

The plot of *Scum* (written by Roy Minton) is set in a British borstal - a young offenders institute run by HM Prison Services. These institutions were intended to "build character" and focused on discipline and authority, but this concept quickly got out of hand and they very often became breeding grounds for abuses of power, bullying and psychopathic behaviour from the screws (the adult warders). In 1983, borstals were reformed and rebranded as Young Offender Institutions. *Scum* deserves much credit for influencing these changes although, as will become apparent, they did not go anywhere near far enough. The film - like the television play - directed by Alan Clarke, debuted on BBC2 that very year and was met with a predictable outcry from Mary Whitehouse and her band of reactionary censors, who, as they often did, went after completely the wrong targets.

Fast forward to 2018 and Minton's script was proved correct when hundreds of former inmates claimed that they had been sexually and physically abused in youth detention centres during the '70s and '80s and called

for a public inquiry. This eventually happened the following year, when it was found that rape, violence and mental torture had been common events in such institutions. The 'short, sharp, shock' tactics of Mrs. Thatcher's Home Secretary, Willie Whitelaw, had only led to horrific abuse, psychological damage and more hardened criminals. Re-offending rates were not improved at all. Naively, most contemporary reviews of Scum seem to state (or infer) that modern British borstals have vastly improved since 1979 and that these institutions are now relatively civilised in comparison. Yet, the 2019 inquiry found that, 40 years after the release of Clarke's incendiary film, abuse of inmates was still a common occurrence. The investigation acknowledged that between 2009 and 2017 more than 1000 sexual attacks on children were reported in these institutions. Out of these, just four had resulted in a conviction (and who knows how many were not reported).

Scum (1977 - the TV Version)

Scum began life in 1977 as a *Play for Today* on BBC1 but was considered too controversial for viewers and banned by the BBC before receiving any screening (it remained unseen on British television until BBC 2 screened an edited version in 1991). Alasdair Milne, then the BBC's Managing Director, and Bill Cotton Jnr, the Controller of BBC1, were behind the ban. After a screening, Cotton reportedly announced: "Over my dead body will this film be shown!"

In early 1978, Milne and Peter Fiddick of the 'Guardian' appeared on the BBC's *Tonight Show* to discuss the banning. Scum had cost the BBC £120,000 of license fee money to make, so the ban required public justification. Milne described the play as "extraordinarily violent" but confessed that he had no idea about what actually went on in modern borstals and appeared to have come to his decision purely due to the fact that he found Scum to be so shockingly realistic and "filmed like a documentary" (which was the point of the piece and Clarke's preferred filming style). Conversely, Fiddick retorted that, to him, it was one of the most compelling pieces of film that British television had ever produced.

The 1977 BBC version of *Scum,* shot in an old people's home in Redhill, features much of the same cast as the film. One notable change was that of Archer. David Threlfall played him in the BBC play but was replaced by Mick Ford for the film. As in the 1979 film, Ray Winstone, then just 19, stars as Carlin, the new inmate who eventually becomes 'the daddy' of his wing. There is marginally less violence and swearing than the feature, but the main difference between *Scum* 1977 and 1979 is the removal from the theatrical version of its homosexual storyline, whereby Carlin takes a younger boy as his 'missus', a perk of his position as the 'daddy'.

Of course, the brutality and racism that so shocked the BBC is exactly what makes it such an important work. Clarke and writer Roy Minton decided that the best way to critique the inherent abuse in the borstal system was to show it. BBC producer Margaret Matheson: "We were very conscious of the fact that it would not be welcomed by the people in authority."

Scum (1977) has since become one of the *cause célèbre* of the British television industry. It joined such works as Peter Watkins' *The War Game* (1965), a brilliant depiction of the after-effects of a nuclear attack on the UK, which, like Clarke's film, blended fiction and documentary techniques and was banned for 20 years. Another example is Dennis Potter's *Brimstone and Treacle* which, like *Scum,*

was recorded for BBC1's *Play for Today* and also deemed too disturbing to broadcast.

What was most upsetting to the powers that be was that the regime of violence, bullying and racism is condoned by the guards and prison directors, who positively encourage it to uphold the hierarchies that emerge. Little wonder then that this stark representation of a system that destroys the weakest and turns the strongest into hardened criminals was seen as too much for a British television audience: too dark, too pessimistic, and most of all, too anti-establishment (Matheson strongly suspected Home Office interference). Yet, the theatrical version would be more violent still…

Scum (1979 - The Feature Film)

In response to the banning of the 1977 version, Matheson organised a screening for the national press in Soho, much to the annoyance of the BBC and resulting in front page headlines. Among the audience was film producer Clive Parsons who was, in his own words "blown away" and (after being rejected by David Puttnam) asked Clarke to re-shoot it as a feature with a budget of £250,000.

Due to the subject matter, finding distribution proved difficult for Parsons. 20th Century Fox and others rejected it outright, so it ended up being independently produced. The production was challenging too. Roy Minton was furious when he got his hands on a shooting script, feeling that his work had been "savaged" by a plethora of scriptwriters with no singular vision. He called Clarke, his long-time collaborator, and they had a vicious row.

Tempers were only cooled when Clive Parsons called a meeting and the script was returned almost completely to its original wording.

Filmed largely in Shenley Psychiatric Hospital, Hertfordshire, *Scum* (1979) focuses on the brutality of a flawed and corrupt system, whereby the inmates have no hope of rehabilitation due to the insanity of the regime. Survival of the fittest seems to literally apply here,

as a system designed to prevent violence only ends up encouraging it in an endless cycle. After hitting a screw, Carlin has been transferred from another borstal (we learn that he was being beaten up and was merely defending himself). He initially declares that he doesn't want any trouble, but after a beating from Pongo Banks and his crew, realises that he'll have to take control of his wing in order to protect himself and get through his sentence. We also bear witness to horrific sexual and violent abuse, racism and two suicides among the other inmates.

Clarke's emphasis on dramatic realism and Phil Méheux's atmospheric cinematography help elevate the film above others in its genre. Shot with an almost Kubrickian eye, the camera moves around with the steadicam menace that would later become Alan Clarke's trademark. The lack of a score, or any form of music to accompany these scenes, makes them feel all the more haunting and prolonged. We never see the outside world, even in the opening prison van scenes, and this emphasises the boys' total isolation. Tension is built over a longer period than the television version and the use of the steadicam (which Clarke also used to similar effect in *Elephant*) allows viewers to follow and become embroiled in the violence - whether they want to or not - whereas the *Play for Today* version is a far more observational affair. Another difference is that the violent aggression and conflict comes more often from the inmates themselves. The key characters of Carlin and Archer are wisely given far more prominence in the theatrical release too.

Winstone's turn as Carlin in the film is now legendary and to this day probably his most iconic role. It's a powerhouse of a performance, perhaps the best he's given bar *Nil by Mouth*. He's perfect: tough, but not without empathy or intelligence, and always looking ready to explode at any second. While there's no doubt that Carlin would have failed any equality and diversity training sessions, he definitely had heart. Ray was cast after Clarke was impressed by the way he walked and his naturally dominating presence, so decided to cast Carlin as a cockney instead of the

GO TO HELL!

scum

SCUM Starring RAY WINSTONE · MICK FORD · JULIAN FIRTH · PHIL DANIELS
Executive Producers DON BOYD and MICHAEL RELPH · Associate Producer MARTIN CAMPBELL
Written by ROY MINTON · Produced by DAVINA BELLING and CLIVE PARSONS
Directed by ALAN CLARKE · A BOYD'S CO. PRODUCTION · COLOR
A WORLD NORTHAL FILM

R RESTRICTED
UNDER 17 REQUIRES ACCOMPANYING PARENT OR ADULT GUARDIAN

intended Glaswegian.

Mick Ford as Archer, the self-styled individual of the inmates, is a revelation. He is my favourite character in the film, who, unlike Carlin's attempts to fight fire with fire, opts for a passive aggressive approach. Archer is smart, sarcastic and determined to be a thorn in the side of the establishment that has held him in the borstal for far too long. He uses no violence but is charismatic and steals every scene he's in. I particularly love his exchange with long-serving screw, Mr. Duke. While the other inmates are in a religious service (Archer is an atheist, though this is more to cause a nuisance to wardens than for any religious convictions), he observes the absurdity of the institution he finds himself in and comments on how Mr. Duke is just as much a prisoner as himself: "You have spent your life in the prison service, yet you are still only a basic officer... now, who gets the stick for that? Us. Who pays for that daily humiliation?" These home-truths infuriate Mr. Duke no end and, unable to handle this discussion intellectually, he puts Archer on report yet again. There's also a nicely observed scene where Archer makes the devout Christian Governor's blood boil, by pretending to be interested in conversion to Islam. The glee on his face as he realises he has gotten under the skin of the borstal's head man is a

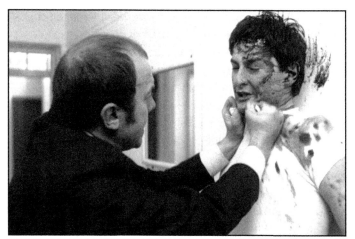

joy to behold.

Aside from the inmates, the wardens/screws are all brilliantly portrayed. None of them have even the slightest bit of sympathy or empathy for their young prisoners and they border on the psychotic. They are a Nazi-like presence throughout and very intimidating, relishing their roles in dehumanising the juvenile offenders under their command. Their normalisation of racism and assault still shock today. In particular, British TV regular John Judd, as Mr. Sands, is state evil personified: a violent, racist and sadistic bully. It's a thoroughly convincing performance. So convincing, in fact, that Winstone reveals in the DVD commentary how he and some of the cast planned to give Judd a beating in the final riot scene. Luckily, he caught wind of this and can be seen on screen darting out of the doors sharpish!

The one-liners in Scum are legion. Carlin's "Where's yer tool?" and "I'm the daddy" being the most well-known, but there are plenty of tasty, quotable lines throughout Minton's meticulously researched and sharp script, and many have real bite. Archer wryly observes: "Sometimes, someday I somehow get the strangest notion they're trying to break my spirit." And, given what we witness, there is no hiding the irony when the Governor declares: "There is no violence here!" The script brings to mind such films as The Loneliness of the Long Distance Runner, If.... and A Clockwork Orange, classic Brit flicks that also held a mirror up to British institutions and raged against the machine.

Winstone actually prefers the 1977 rendering of Scum:

"I really liked the original, because we were younger, there was something about that that made it seem more violent, more terrifying. We were vulnerable kids, being abused by men and then abusing each other - in every way, violently, mentally, sexually, the lot in a fucking Victorian building. We were kids in the feature films but in two years we grew up, we weren't so vulnerable anymore." He also later regretted the deletion of his character's homosexual scene in the theatrical release. A decision which he had agreed with when making the feature, regretfully stating that he was feeling "*too macho*" at the time of filming. A consequence of the removal of Carlin's '*missus*' is a tougher performance from Winstone and a stronger focus on violence and male toxicity. This change caused Minton and Clarke to have a huge falling out (they didn't reconcile until Alan was dying in hospital 11 years later). Minton felt passionately that the original script was stronger, as it made Carlin vulnerable in an institution where he could not afford to be vulnerable.

Scum eventually premiered to a packed screening at The Prince Charles Cinema, London on the 20th September, 1979. Reviews were strong and it performed very well in Britain, despite (or because of) the usual controversies that surrounded the subject matter. It was different in other territories though. Clive Parsons felt it almost impossible to market abroad, especially in the US, where it was misunderstood by distributors and considered an arthouse film. Over the years, *Scum* gained a large cult following on video and then DVD, with Carlin and many of his iconic lines now firmly established in British popular culture. The 1977 BBC play was finally released in 2004 in a special double DVD that contained both versions. On the commentary, Winstone, having not seen the 1979 film for years, seems surprised at how powerful *Scum* remains and states: "I'm very, very proud of it" before declaring that he wants to watch it again that evening. Many would agree, with *Dog Pound* (2010) being the most obvious of the many movies to be influenced by it.

All these years later, both the 1977 and the 1979 interpretations of *Scum* remain powerful, emotive experiences and I admire them equally. Suicide, rape, extreme brutality, corruption and racism are not shied away from.

However, I do find the 1979 film's finale a touch more powerfully executed than the TV version. A sudden cut from the rioting visually shows how the system reasserts itself and the cycle begins again. It's a thoroughly depressing but thoughtful conclusion that will remain with you long after the silent end credits roll.

Clarke's work is rebellious, raw and thought-provoking, but never preachy. As in *Scum*, he often championed the ignored, the underprivileged and the institutionalised. Clarke showed an empathy for them that was severely lacking in almost every other modern director's work. Each of his films still sizzle with pent-up anger and frustration at the inequality of '70s and '80s Britain. His message was simple: this is how bad things really are, now what are you going to do about it?

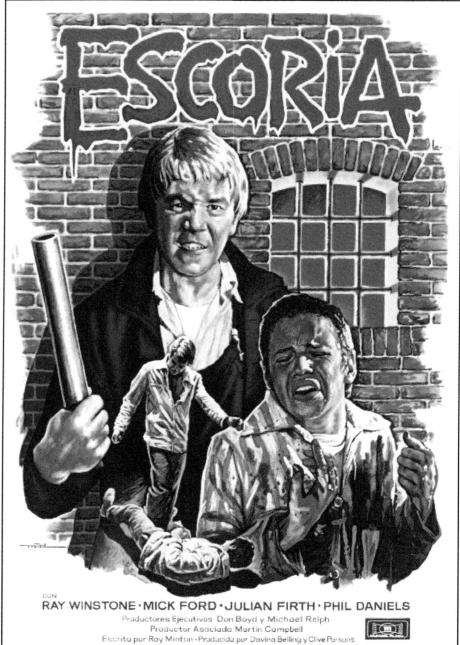

CON
RAY WINSTONE · MICK FORD · JULIAN FIRTH · PHIL DANIELS
Productores Ejecutivos Don Boyd y Michael Relph
Productor Asociado Martin Campbell
Escrita por Roy Minton · Producida por Davina Belling y Clive Parsons
Dirigida por Alan Clarke · Color

Caine-ing the Financial Caper

SILVER BEARS

by Ian Talbot Taylor

Silver Bears was a British-funded movie that appeared in 1977, when London-born star Michael Caine was still early into his slightly awkward Hollywood stage which would include a clutch of sub-standard disaster epics. It can easily be filed within a large folder of fairly forgotten productions that see the iconic actor wearing smart blazers and sharply creased flares as he saunters around a variety of European (and further afield) locations. Like the previous decade's *The Italian Job* (1969), it is a crime caper, offering a mixture of drama and mild chuckles, but Caine himself had already started transforming from the lean, young cheeky Cockney into a blockier man of middle-age. There is much less action here too, and it is easy to understand how and why *Silver Bears* is less remembered than *The Italian Job*. But that doesn't make it a bad film. It is a very interesting one, in fact, although the original writer's story is perhaps more interesting still.

'The Silver Bears', the original novel, was written by Paul Emil Erdman, an American (though Canadian-born) economist and banker who was successful in writing novels based on monetary trends and international finance.

Born in 1932, Erdman graduated first with a Bachelor of Divinity Degree in 1954, having studied at both the Concordia Seminary and the School of Foreign Service at Georgetown University. He then received a PHD in Economics, European History and Theology from Switzerland's University of Basel in 1958. Apparently, the publication of his thesis provoked the ire of the Swiss government as it revealed aspects of Nazi clients that had done business with Swiss banks!

Between 1958 and the late '60s/early '70s, Erdman worked as a financial analyst and economist before becoming the president of a Swiss bank. However, the bank collapsed after a deal in the cocoa market went sour and he and other board members were accused of fraud and mismanagement. Erdman spent ten months in solitary confinement but was eventually released in 1971 without charge on a $133,000 bail bond. He skipped bail and laid low in England, although he later returned to America. Along with other bank officials, Erdman was convicted and served time in jail. He eventually received a nine-year sentence in absentia.

It was during his prison time that Erdman eked out his time by taking up writing. Of course, he was somewhat restricted as regards being able to conduct research and so he stuck to fiction and adopted the wise old advice of writing about what he knew. Thus, he created what has since become known as the financial thriller, starting with 'The Billion Dollar Sure Thing' (1973, UK title 'The Billion Dollar Killing') which won a 1974 Edgar Award from the Mystery Writers of America for Best First Novel. Erdman would continue to write novels until the year of his death in 2007. The second in the run was the 1974 publication 'The Silver Bears', which is where we came in…

The movie adaption lost the definite article, becoming just *Silver Bears*. Erdman's intricately plotted tale about making a fortune, not necessarily legitimately, via banks and silver mines, was well received. 'Kirkus' called it "another assured jackpot for an unnumbered account of readers." The plot follows a Mafia family (run by Martin Balsam in initially gregarious fashion, playing his first scene in a hot tub full of fleshy middle-aged mobsters with wobbly, naked buttocks!) that is keen to establish an efficient money-laundering organization. To do so, they acquire a Swiss bank, and Balsam sends one of his most solid, dependables, a financial expert - Caine as Doc Fletcher - to oversee operations. But their not-quite-legitimate enterprise involves a small, shabby bank on the first floor above a pizza parlour and is complicated by the schemes of a billionaire American speculator living in England, a couple of smugglers running an illicit Iranian silver mine, and a scam that could collapse the entire international monetary system.

Caine is his usual unflappable self. Even when things go wrong (as they absolutely must do if this sort of caper is to hold the viewer's interest) he remains admirably low key yet confident. He might show a tightness of the collar with a small gesture, there might be the slightest change in the angle of his head as he looks at people, and yes, he might raise his voice, but he is still physically in control. Caine is the last word in economical acting to monumental effect.

Early scenes make the most of the fantastic Swiss scenery expertly captured by Anthony B. Richmond. Cinematographer Richmond had previously photographed Caine in the previous year's *The Eagle Has Landed* though his earlier '70s jobs ranged from the sublime (*Don't Look Now*) to the ridiculous (*Vampira*), something that foreshadowed the rest of his busy career.

Claude Bolling provides a jazzy, funky and glamorous opening score that suits the early Las Vegas scenes perfectly, changing subtly enough to cover what amounts to a travelogue reel of Swiss banks which still remains jaunty. The audience is never left in any doubt that for all the potential jeopardy hovering above the principal characters, this is still a movie intended to tickle as much as thrill. It is a relatively swift-moving bank caper and flip-flopping sting escapade - almost bewilderingly so - with perhaps too many faces (many familiar) appearing one after the other in the first ten minutes.

Critics were unsure. 'Time Out' said: "Paul Erdman's 'The Silver Bears', an amusing novel about high finance and high-level chicanery, becomes a film about lowest common denominators and low-level buffoonery."

True enough, the humour does indeed lean a little bit

towards the wacky side. Initially Caine swaggers into the wrong bank, trying (and almost succeeding) in taking over a big, plush affair. When he finally finds the correct establishment, he finds it to be a disappointing, untidy little place above the previously mentioned pizza parlour.

'Time Out' singled out the director Ivan Passer and writer Peter Stone when specifying what was wrong with the film. "Passer brings to the subject all the subtle wit of 'Pravda', and scriptwriter Peter Stone fumbles it by being both confusing and condescending." This is perhaps overly harsh. American screenwriter and playwright Stone either wrote or co-wrote the screenplays for the mid-1960s hits *Charade* (1963), *Father Goose* (1964), and (an Oscar winner for him) *Mirage* (1965), all of which showcased his ability to present lightly amusing situations and dialogue. What's more, in 1974 he wrote the screenplay for *The Taking of Pelham 123*, clearly highlighting his ability to create high class thrills.

Perhaps the Czech director, Passer was a more unlikely choice for *Silver Bears*, having been associated with the Czechoslovakian New Wave of cinema. He attended school with fellow Czech filmmaker Miloš Forman, and although he failed to finish his course at FAMU (the Film and TV School of the Academy of Performing Arts in Prague) he was able to find work and, in fact, worked with his friend on all of Forman's Czech films, including *Loves of a Blonde* (1965) and *The Firemen's Ball* (1967), both co-written by Passer and nominated for Academy Awards. Nevertheless, he was best known for his work on gritty dramas and not comedy vehicles. *Silver Bears* simply does not feel like a good fit.

One feels that it is the all-star cast that really injects the life and wackiness into proceedings. Then again, 'Time Out' had it in for the players too! "... the really insuperable burden is the feeble pack of turns from the cast (they can't be called performances): Caine as

the financial wizard, [Stéphane] Audran as a woman who wears lots of different clothes, and [Louis] Jourdan doing his professional European act. Worst is Cybill Shepherd as a kind of giggling California wholefood cereal, wearing layers of woollens and layers of spectacles. If your idea of a good laugh is watching Caine spill his breakfast onto his lap - twice in a row - this is your movie."

If the criticisms of the writer and director were perhaps overly harsh then this slating of the cast is most definitely so. Caine is Caine, but that in itself is an absolute plus. And surely the whole point of hiring Jourdan is to have him play a Euro aristocrat? Audran is actually charming and funny, no more so than when she and Jourdan develop a romantic attraction based upon slapping each other! Perhaps of its time and made more palatable by Audran's shocked reaction to her own striking of Jourdan. She also plays well off her fellow con artist David Warner who (as often happened in the '70s) pulls off the cool, hippy playboy look. That man Warner had range! As for Cybill Shepherd, trying to find her career path post-*The Last Picture Show* (1971) and *Taxi Driver* (1976). It could be that her delightfully dotty and frothy performance as Debbie Luckman, the wife of one of Caine's rivals, gave her some ideas. She borders on tongue-in-cheek slapstick silliness and although the character is way different, it's surely not too many steps away from the role of Maddy in '80s television hit *Moonlighting*.

Add to all this, performances of interest from great British character actors like Charles Gray and Joss Ackland to names most often associated away from dramatic performances - I'm talking about musical comedian Tom Smothers as Shepherd's husband and talk show host Jay Leno as a giggling gangster of the good though goonish variety latterly - and you've got a movie that has plenty to sustain one's interest.

Is the cast the most interesting thing about it? Well, yes, probably, and is Erdman's original novel superior, definitely. Still, *Silver Bears* is a decent enough time-killer, a crime caper that will never gain as much love as Caine's more famous *The Italian Job* but will reward the viewer and do so whilst looking rather classy. Caine's best Hollywood material would arguably start arriving in the next decade (along with some undoubted dross) and his British '70s movies eclipsed his US excursions, but this one deserves a chance. It's only about a swindle, trust me, you won't feel cheated.

The money is hot... The tricksters are cool...
And the comedy is quick-silver fast!

Nat Cohen presents an Alex Winitsky and Arlene Sellers Production

MICHAEL CAINE - CYBILL SHEPHERD
LOUIS JOURDAN - STEPHANE AUDRAN
DAVID WARNER - TOM SMOTHERS and
MARTIN BALSAM as Fiore

$ILVER BEAR$

Music by CLAUDE BOLLING · Executive Producer MARTIN C. SCHUTE · Based on the novel by PAUL ERDMAN
Screenplay by PETER STONE · Produced by ARLENE SELLERS and ALEX WINITSKY
Directed by IVAN PASSER   Technicolor   Distributed by EMI Films Limited

EMI   AFB

LE MAGNIFIQUE

by Jonathon Dabell

Anyone watching *Le Magnifique* (1973) for the first time might be caught off guard by the opening twenty minutes. During that stretch, outlandish and preposterous events come thick and fast yet all seem to be played deadpan, unfathomably straight. The very first scene - set in Acapulco, Mexico - shows a secret agent making a call, but the telephone box in which he stands is abruptly hoisted into the air by a giant mechanical claw dangling from the underside of a helicopter. It is then dropped from a great height into the sea, agent still inside, and the poor chap is promptly devoured by a shark. Another secret agent - the cooler-than-cool, infallible, indestructible Bob St. Clare (Jean-Paul Belmondo) - is sent to Mexico to find out who killed his ill-fated colleague. He is handed this new assignment during a frantic fistfight, holding a phone to his ear while using furniture, fists and the phone itself to beat off wave after wave of opponents. Once in Mexico, the madcap mayhem continues - our hero meets his contact Tatiana (Jacqueline Bisset), casually shoots assassins and ambushers as they drive from the airport, and accidentally drops a cyanide pill into the hotel pool, killing several guests. Later, when they are attacked on the beach by an army of enemy frogmen, St. Clare and Tatiana take cover in nearby rocks and use pistols against their enemies. Each bullet they fire takes down four or five of the oncoming foes. It's gloriously silly, violent, over-the-top, incoherent and entertaining, all at once, but tonally it's hard to tell where the film is going or what it is trying to achieve.

We finally realise what's going on around the twenty-minute mark when a cleaning lady walks through the middle of this ferocious gunfight on the beach, guiding a switched-on hoover in front of her while heading toward a doorway positioned incongruously in the middle of the golden sand. The exotic Mexican coast fades from view as she passes through the door and in its place we see an author, Francois Merlin (Belmondo again), sitting at a typewriter in a messy, drab apartment, trying to ignore the noisy arrival of his cleaning lady. He is hitting the keys hard, desperately trying to get the words on paper before he forgets them. He bears a resemblance to the heroic superspy St. Clare, but his hair is messier, his looks less refined, his surroundings decidedly less glamorous. We realise at once that he is a novelist; the rather bonkers 20-minute action sequence we have just watched is his latest story as envisaged by him as he types it onto the page.

The switch is neat and well-timed. It arrives just as we - the viewers - are beginning to question what we are watching. Until now, the film has come across like a James Bond-style spy story with an Inspector Clouseau-like superspy for its hero, set against exotic locales and populated with scores of beautiful women. But once we're introduced to Merlin in his gloomy apartment - appearance dishevelled, chain-smoking while attempting to fill his page with words - we become aware that this is actually the story of an overworked and underpaid pulp writer who imagines a more exciting existence for himself through his stories. So, yes, it is a spy spoof, but it's also much more than that. Not only does it deconstruct and affectionately mock the spy genre, it also deconstructs and affectionately mocks those who write such stories in the first place.

As the film progresses, we come back to Bob St. Clare's adventures from time to time but the final 80 minutes or so of *Le Magnifique* concerns itself much more with the character of Francois Merlin. We learn that he bases the locations in his novels on photographs, magazines and brochures lying around his living room. Similarly, he bases his fictional characters on people from the real world. So, for example, when a pair of useless electricians come to Merlin's apartment and refuse to carry out the urgent repairs he needs over health and safety concerns, he then incorporates two identical characters into his story as villainous lackeys. The main antagonist in his latest novel - an Albanian supervillain name Karpov - is fashioned after his arrogant, greedy, womanising editor Pierre Charron (Vittorio Caprioli) who constantly refuses to extend deadlines, pay advances or help Merlin in any way.

The backbone of the entire film comes from Merlin's attraction to a new English neighbour living in his apartment block. Christine (Bisset again), a sociology student, occasionally passes Merlin on the stairwell or shares an elevator with him down to the ground floor. If he positions his typewriter just right, he can catch fleeting glimpses of her moving across her apartment on the

storey above. Christine has no idea Merlin knows who she is, nor that he has even noticed her, but the truth of the matter is that in his hopelessly romantic mind he is head-over-heels in love with her. It is no surprise, therefore, that the character of Tatiana in his latest novel is entirely based on Christine.

The Bob St. Clare episodes become increasingly linked to the events in Merlin's life. When things are going well between Merlin and Christine in real life, things go well between St. Clare and Tatiana on the printed page. When Merlin believes Christine might be having a fling with his editor Charron, he writes an entire sequence where she is abused and humiliated by dozens of Albanian soldiers (the scene is depicted comically, not graphically). When Merlin's mood is low, St. Clare is shown as a reclusive ex-agent living in exile and suffering from a heavy cold. When he rediscovers his vim and verve, the scenes showing him in a depressed funk play in reverse and the character reverts to his old confident, cocky, indestructible self.

Le Magnifique works beautifully on two levels. As a spoof, it is inspired. As a romantic drama, it has real warmth and heart.

A brilliantly funny scene involves the capture of an Albanian agent, mortally wounded. St. Clare orders

someone to fetch a translator so the wounded man can be interrogated before he dies. A line of five men file sombrely into the interrogation room, and the first explains: "I found an Albanian interpreter but he only knows Romanian. So, we had to find a Romanian but he only knows Serbian. The Serb only knows Russian, and the Russian only knows Czech. Fortunately, I speak Czech!" "It will take us a lot of time!" observes St. Clare's colleague. Before they've even managed to send one question along the line and the corresponding reply back to the first translator, the victim is dead.

The wistful romance between Merlin and Christine is a joy. Belmondo shows a terrific flare for slapstick in the fictional episodes, not entirely dissimilar to what Peter

Sellers brought to the role of Inspector Clouseau, and Bisset proves a surprisingly good comedienne as his comic foil. But in their dramatic real-world scenes, they are even better. We long for them to end up together, but their road to mutual happiness is bumpy, taking several twists and turns before reaching its conclusion. Belmondo has charm, charisma and Gallic good looks in abundance; Bisset looks better than she has ever looked on screen in an array of amazing outfits, glamorous and sizzling as Tatiana, sweet and bookish as Christine. In fact, director Philippe de Broca deserves credit for eliciting fine performances from all his cast, not just the leads.

The sun-soaked, exotic beauty of the scenes set in bookworld contrast brilliantly with those which take place in the real world, where rooms look messy, characters appear stressed/tired/scruffy, and the weather is usually grey and rainy. Claude Bolling's lovely score captures these various moods and styles perfectly.

Le Magnifique (also known as *The Man from Acapulco* and, rather clunkily, *How to Destroy the Reputation of the Greatest Secret Agent*) is a joy, a comedy-drama which leaves you with a big, silly, sloppy grin on your face as the credits roll. The original title translates literally as "The Magnificent", and nothing could be more apt.

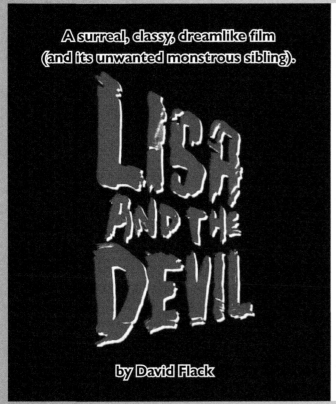

A surreal, classy, dreamlike film (and its unwanted monstrous sibling).

LISA AND THE DEVIL

by David Flack

I am a big fan of the Italian director Mario Bava. I love the way his films were made, his unique style, his use of colour, his genius in turning out something worthwhile on a budget so low it would cripple most filmmakers. Why, then, did I hesitate when I was asked to write about Bava's *Lisa and the Devil* for 'Cinema of the '70s' Issue 10? Read on, dear reader, and find out.

The film wastes no time getting down to things. After a nice opening titles sequence featuring playing cards, we cut straight to a tourist bus arriving in the Spanish city of Toledo. During the tour, the visitors are taken to a fresco on a wall which shows the face of Satan. One tourist, our heroine Lisa (Elke Sommer), wanders into a shop where she is startled to see a beret-wearing man who has the same face as the devil depicted on the old fresco. Sensing her uneasiness, he attempts to appease her with a big smile, but she remains unsettled since he seems to be in the process of purchasing a lifelike mannequin. She wanders off in a daze and is terrified when a man who looks just like the mannequin approaches and accosts her. Lisa struggles and the man falls down a flight of stairs and is killed. She panics and becomes disorientated, losing her way. She stumbles across a chauffeur-driven car and begs for a lift which the couple occupying it reluctantly give. The car breaks down and they go to a nearby villa to use the phone. The door is answered by the butler Leandro (Telly Savalas) who is the same man Lisa saw buying the mannequin in the shop. He informs them there is not a phone but invites them in. Inside they meet Maximilian (Alessio Orano) whose mother, a blind Countess (Alida Valli), owns the property. Maximilian asks his mother if

the visitors can stay overnight. She reluctantly agrees… and so begins a strange night of madness, dark secrets, manipulation and murder.

The plot isn't exactly original, but the film has a strong dreamlike feel especially in the opening sequences. The villa's multi-layered corridors enhance the dream effect. There is a simple, effective shock moment early on, during a dinner scene, which shows Bava's playfulness. There are also subtle nods to his previous films such as *Kill, Baby, Kill* (1966) and *Hatchet for the Honeymoon* (1970), while the mother and son characters have a *Psycho* vibe about them. The murder scenes are (for the time) quite gory and effectively done. Watching it again in preparation for this article, I'd forgotten how brutal these scenes are. They definitely add to the constant sense of uneasiness and stay in the memory long after the film has ended. There's also a scene which a few years later would become something of a horror cliché, showing dead people sitting at a dinner table (a visual shock repeated in several '80s slashers).

The biggest example of Bava's playfulness and cleverness is in the character of Leandro the butler.

Seemingly mostly in the background, he does very little but it is very clear he is the puppetmaster, imperceptibly pulling strings and engineering everything that happens. Smug, confident, decidedly odd and extremely manipulative, he adds to our growing unease and we are aware throughout that he is completely in control. This sense of sinisterness is difficult to explain to anyone who hasn't seen the film, but it is heightened by things like Leandro's odd habit of walking around with lifelike mannequins, shrugging it off as an act of eccentricity, and the little everyday servant chores he performs which never seem quite right. A lot of what Lisa experiences doesn't make sense (like in a dream) and it all lends a disorientating, bewildering, nightmarish quality. Familiar elements are thrown in (reincarnated lover, dark secrets, insanity, etc.) and the whole experience makes for an odd, interesting watch with several effective scenes which really stay with you afterwards. It's a surreal, classy chiller with giallo and traditional horror elements. The final scene has a neat twist, just as you would expect from a devil with an artistic bent.

Now, I mentioned at the start that I'd hesitated when first approached to write about this film and I feel I should explain why. My main reservation was that it bought back a horrid memory of an atrocity called *The House of Exorcism*, a widely derided re-edit of the film which came out in 1975.

When first released, *Lisa and the Devil* wasn't a box office success. In fact, it struggled to attract much interest from distributors at all. Then the phenomenon that was *The Exorcist* hit screens in 1973, resulting in a spate of rip-offs being churned out in quick succession. Alfred Leone, the producer of *Lisa and the Devil*, was envious of the money these cheapjack knock-offs were making so he persuaded Bava to film some new footage featuring Sommer and Robert Alda (father of Alan) and to incorporate a new possession subplot to the story. The new scenes were edited into existing scenes from *Lisa and the Devil* and the resulting hodge-podge was issued under the title *The House of Exorcism*. To be fair, Leone's idea worked on a commercial level with this new cut proving a box office success. The downside was that it was awful, a shameless rip-off of *The Exorcist* incorporating many scenes from *Lisa* but using the new stuff to alter the core plot into something very different. Additional scenes included some fashionable vomiting (one scene depicts someone throwing up frogs!) and coarse, crude language.

The new material is very poor at best. When Bava saw *The House of Exorcism*, he was rightly appalled and it affected him deeply. He asked to have his name removed from the credits, and Leone took over the remaining directorial chores, crediting himself as Micky Leone in the opening credits. I saw this atrocity before I saw Bava's original version, and for that reason I avoided seeing *Lisa and the Devil* in its original form for many years because I was scarred by the sheer terribleness of the re-cut version. I'm glad I finally gave it a chance, as it is now my third favourite Bava film! I only saw the monstrous offshoot once (frankly, once more than I should have!) Both versions were on the DVD I used for this review, and I quickly skimmed through a few scenes of the re-edit and shuddered (not in a good way). In my honest opinion, it shouldn't even be classed as a Bava film.

Lisa and the Devil boasts a strong cast. Heading things

is Sommer as the titular Lisa Reiner. She had played the heroine in Bava's *Baron Blood* (1972) and proves a capable lead here. She was a seasoned pro, appearing in over a hundred films in various genres. Savalas, playing Leandro (the strange butler/devil figure), really enjoys himself, giving a magnetic performance which is one of the best of his career. It's hard to imagine anyone being more effective in the role. Mysterious, confident and sinister, he is a major factor in everything that works with this movie. His career as a solid character-actor was about to take a big boost as the TV series *Kojak* (1973-1978), in which he played a lollipop-sucking detective, was just around the corner.

Sylva Koscina plays Sophia Lehar, one half of the troubled couple that give Lisa the fated ride. She has secrets of her own and features in one memorable wince-inducing scene. She appeared in many genres and had a solid career in sword-and-sandal, war, giallo, spy, comedy and thriller films. Her rich husband Francis is played by veteran Spanish actor Eduardo Fajardo. He'd appeared in many movies, making his debut as far back as 1947 (in fact, he appeared in 8 films that year!), before carving out a prolific career in mostly Spanish or Italian films often in villainous cowboy roles. Both Koscina and Fajardo do solid work here.

Orano has a prominent role as Maximilian, the Countess' son, in only his fourth film. He didn't have a particularly long or varied career thereafter but is very competent in a role which reminds me strongly of Stephen Forsyth's character in Bava's *Hatchet for the Honeymoon* (1970). Valli get a significant part too as the mysterious Countess. The Italian actress had already enjoyed a long career, working for Alfred Hitchcock and Carol Reed back in the '40s (*The Paradine Case* and *The Third Man* respectively). She too does good work in *Lisa and the Devil*. A mention is in order lastly for Gabrielle Tinti who plays George, the ill-fated chauffeur, adding another enjoyable characterisation

to his long and varied resumé.

Lisa and the Devil consolidates Bava's status as my favourite Italian director, well ahead of other popular choices like Dario Argento, Lucio Fulci and Sergio Leone. He was credited with 79 film and TV episodes (and countless uncredited assignments) in many genres, but it's for his work in the horror/fantasy genre that he is most well known. He was also credited as the 'Father' of the giallo genre. My personal favourites of his are *Black Sabbath* (1963), *The Whip and the Body* (1963), *Lisa and the Devil*, *Rabid Dogs* (1974) (covered by me in Issue 3 of 'Cinema of the '70s) and, perhaps his most famous film, *Black Sunday* (1960). I admire many of his films including ones I have not shortlisted here. He considered the original cut of *Lisa and the Devil* a good film, something to be proud of, but was deeply affected and upset by the *House of Exorcism* debacle. It caused him to grow increasingly cynical about the film business and he only completed two more films, *Rabid Dogs* and *Shock* (1977), before dying in 1980 at the age of 65.

Lisa and the Devil has been somewhat under-rated and underseen until recent years, largely because of the lousy reputation of *The House of Exorcism*. It is finally more widely available in its proper form, and has gradually earned the praise it deserves. I'm sure Bava (repose bene maestro) would be happy with that.

40

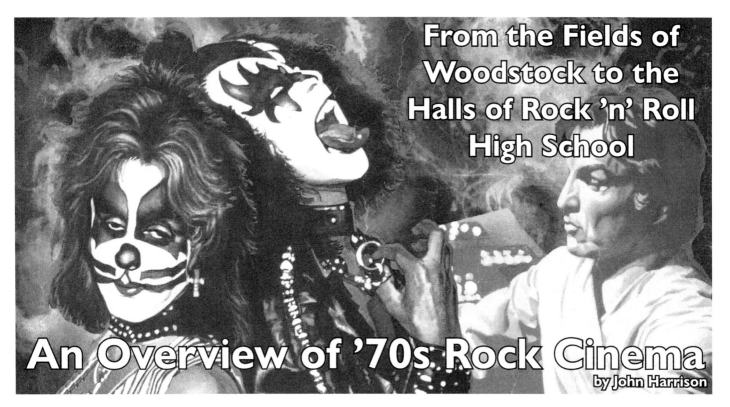

Once rock and roll music began to spark a raging wildfire amongst American youth in the mid '50s, it didn't take filmmakers very long at all to start exploiting this wild new form of musical expression that many thought was no doubt a passing fad. After all, it was the perfect subject to exploit: it was loved by both boys and girls, movies revolving around it could be made cheap, and the music was being associated with many of the elements that were essential for drive-in fodder: drug use, juvenile delinquency, fast cars and making-out (if not indulging in actual pre-marital sex).

The '60s continued the trend, with the *Beach Party* movies starring Frankie Avalon and Annette Funicello, seemingly unending Elvis flicks, and The Beatles in the brilliant *A Hard Day's Night* (1964) and its inferior (though still fascinating) follow-ups. But by the late '60s, rock and roll wasn't so simple anymore. It had branched out into many diverse sub-genres, from pop and soul to acid and hard rock. It created a more fertile ground for filmmakers entering the new decade, and the '70s would begin with two milestone documentaries which covered two enormous outdoor rock events that ended up being the perfect, though polar opposite, exclamation marks to finish off the '60s.

Michael Wadleigh's *Woodstock* (1970) was a three-hour-plus documentation of the counterculture's watershed moment, the three-day Woodstock Music and Art Festival which took place near Bethel in New York during August 15-18, 1969. Among the people who helped edit the massive amount of footage together - which included performances by the Who, Jefferson Airplane, Santana and Jimi Hendrix - was a young Martin Scorsese, as well as his own future long-term editor Thelma Schoonmaker. Produced for a reasonable $600,000, *Woodstock* the movie would go on to be almost as big a phenomenon as the event itself, eventually grossing over $50 million in the US alone. A 25th anniversary director's cut was released in 1994 and added over 40 minutes of new footage.

At the opposite end of the spectrum, but no less important or impactful, was *Gimme Shelter* (1970), a documentary co-directed by Charlotte Zwerin and brothers Albert and David Maysles, which chronicled the final weeks of The Rolling Stones' now-mythical 1969 American tour, which culminated in a huge, hastily organised free concert at the Altamont Speedway racetrack in northern California on December 6, 1969. Stones frontman Mick Jagger wanted the free concert to be his own Woodstock, which had taken place just several months earlier. But while Woodstock mostly held up its values of peace and love, Altamont would be quickly enveloped by a cloud of gloom and a pervading atmosphere of terror, which reached a peak when Meredith Hunter, an African American who was in the audience, was stabbed to death by a member of the Hell's Angels just a few feet away from where Jagger was performing during the Stones' set. For some reason, the organisers thought it would be a good idea to hire members of the Hell's Angels motorcycle gang to provide security at the event, and then had the bright idea to pay them in beer.

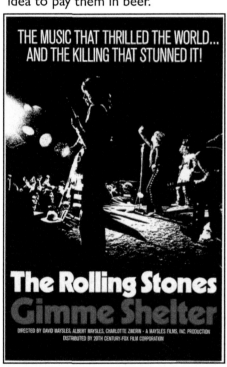

Interspersed with some electrifying performances from the Stones at Madison Square Gardens, as well as a visit to the famous Muscle Shoals recording studio in Alabama (where the band worked on their upcoming *Sticky Fingers* album), *Gimme Shelter* masterfully builds a growing sense of tension and gloom, culminating in the fatal knife attack, which the documentary cameras captured in harrowing detail. Coming not long after the Manson Family killing shocked America and the world with its lurid media stories of a crazed hippie cult on an LSD-fuelled murder spree, Altamont seemed like a final nail in the coffin of the mythical "peace and love" ideology of the '60s counterculture, and *Gimme Shelter* captures its death knell with devastating potency.

When the Stones undertook their next American tour in 1972, in support of their *Exile on Main St.* album, they brought along Swiss documentarian Robert Frank, whose grainy, black and white cinema vérité cameras captured footage that the band felt was so salacious and potentially damaging that they filed a court injunction to stop the completed film, salaciously titled *Cocksucker Blues* (1972), from ever being seen or released. Featuring footage of various band members and personnel doing drugs (everything from pot to cocaine to heroin), groupies and road crew cavorting on

the band's private plane, and Keith Richards enjoying a nice H-induced nod, it was not a side of the Stones that the band wanted depicted on film, especially with the Altamont tragedy still fresh in peoples' minds. *Cocksucker Blues* was shelved and subsequently became one of the most sought-after rock bootleg VHS tapes in the '80s. In its place, the Stones released a more traditional live concert film, *Ladies and Gentlemen: The Rolling Stones* (1974).

Before they became the domain of MTV, cable television specials, and home video, the '70s would see a number of live rock concert films released to the cinema. The huge screens and big stereo sound systems made them an experience for the audience, many of whom no doubt showed up in various altered states of mind! Amongst some of the better and more memorable concert films from the decade are, *Elvis On Tour* (1972), *Ziggy Stardust and the Spiders from Mars* (1973), Alice Cooper's *Welcome to My Nightmare* (1975), Led Zeppelin's *The Song Remains the Same* (1976), and of course, Martin Scorsese's influential classic *The Last Waltz* (1978), which captured the final concert by The Band and included guest appearances by Bob Dylan, Eric Clapton and many

others. Many concert films also included backstage and behind-the-scenes segments showing rehearsals, media promotional appearances, etc., while some, like *Welcome to My Nightmare* and *The Song Remains the Same* had studio-shot fantasy sequences added to them, to make them an even trippier experience for the audience. In a whole world of its own was Frank Zappa's *200 Motels* (1971), which combined live musical performances with surrealist vignettes filled with solar flares, multi-exposures and other optical effects, and was the first feature film to be shot entirely on videotape (which was then subsequently transferred to 35mm film).

The burgeoning nostalgia for pre-Beatles American rock and roll that was already brewing in the early '70s was showcased to near-perfection in George Lucas' sophomore feature *American Graffiti* (1973) which followed a group of recent high school graduates and their adventures over a single Californian night in the summer of 1962. Featuring an outstanding young cast that includes Ron Howard, Candy Clark, Richard Dreyfuss, Cindy Williams and Harrison Ford, the film's potent period atmosphere was powered along by a soundtrack brimming with original classic hits by Chuck Berry, Buddy Holly & the Crickets, The Beach Boys, Bill Haley & the Comets, The Big Bopper, Del Shannon and many more. Lucas spent so much money clearing the rights to use all the songs that he had no budget left over for any traditional score, but the move certainly paid off, with the double-album soundtrack selling over three million copies in America alone. *American Graffiti* would also exert a clear influence of the hit television sit-com *Happy Days*, which ran for ten years from 1974 and also starred Ron Howard in the lead role.

In the UK, rock and roll nostalgia was also a strong presence in *That'll Be the Day* (1973), a coming-of-age

drama starring Rosemary Leach and real-life rock stars David Essex, Adam Faith, Ringo Starr, Keith Moon, Dave Edmunds and Billy Fury. Set primarily in the late '50s and early '60s, the film depicts the adventures of an intelligent but restless youth (Essex) being raised by a single mum (Leach) in urban England, who drops out of school and immerses himself in the rock and roll lifestyle while working at seaside resorts and funfairs. *That'll Be the Day* was a lot grimier than *American Graffiti*, but was likewise driven by a soundtrack of great, mostly American '50s rock, though Billy Fury also contributed a few tracks. The soundtrack spent seven straight weeks at the top of the UK album charts, and the film itself was one of the biggest hits of the year in that country, prompting a sequel the following year. *Stardust* (1974) was only the second feature directed by Michael Apted, and saw David Essex return as his Jim MacLaine character, as we witness his rise and fall as a member

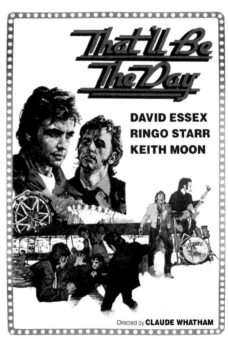

of the rock group the Stray Cats, whom he works for initially as a road manager before he takes over as their lead singer and centre of attention. Like *That'll Be the Day*, *Stardust* also featured a soundtrack stacked with classic hits, this time focusing on the '60s and incorporating everything from vocal pop to the psychedelic and protest rock that emerged later in the decade.

Another interesting UK production featuring former Beatle Ringo Starr (who had also appeared in *200 Motels*) was *Son of Dracula* (1974). Directed by the oft-brilliant Freddie Francis and billed as "The world's first rock and roll Dracula movie," the film

was also co-produced by Starr and distributed through Apple Films, the cinema branch of the creative business empire which the Beatles established in 1968. Set in contemporary England, *Son of Dracula* stars singer-songwriter Harry Nilsson as Count Downe, son of the infamous Count Dracula himself. Arriving in England so he can be crowned as some sort of "Overlord of the Underworld," and accompanied by his assistant and astrologer Merlin the Magician (Starr), Count Downe prefers to spend his time jamming with his rock and roll band, The Count Downes. When he falls in love with a beautiful blonde mortal woman (Suzanna Leigh), he seeks out old family nemesis Van Helsing (Dennis Price) in a bid to have his vampirism reversed.

As a horror-comedy, *Son of Dracula* is at best an interesting misfire... the troubled production saw Freddie Francis give up on it during the editing phase, and Monty Python's Graham Chapman was later brought in to write some new dialogue to be dubbed into it in order for it to make more sense (or at least be funnier). The film though barely saw release and has never officially appeared on home video, but is still worth watching for its horror homages, appearances by Peter Frampton, John Bonham, and Keith Moon as members of The Count Downes, and of course the great Nilsson songs performed throughout. Most of the

tracks were taken from Nilsson's two most recent albums, *Nilsson Schmilsson* and *Son of Schmilsson*, along with one new number, *Daybreak*. The soundtrack to *Son of Dracula* - which also included sound effects and snippets of dialogue - was originally released in a cool die-cut triple gatefold sleeve, which would fold out into a large bat shape, with a collage of black and white photos on one side (some early presses also included an iron-on transfer).

The satirical fantasy was another popular sub-genre of '70s rock cinema, highlighted by Russ Meyer's delirious pop masterpiece *Beyond the Valley of the Dolls* (1970), featuring the fictional all-girl trio The Carrie Nations and their rise to fame - and the trappings and excess that it brings - amongst the happening music L.A. music scene (see 'Cinema of the '70s' #9 David Michael Brown's excellent detailed article on this film). *Slade in Flame* (1975) was fascinating in that it starred a real-life band, the popular UK glam rock outfit Slade, as a fictional band called Flame, who rise to the top of the '60s music scene with help from a marketing company, only to disintegrate and split while at the height of their success. Though it depicted the usual rise and fall story in many ways, *Slade in Flame* did so in a way that was often inventively satirical, and had a darker tone to it

than the generally feel-good party music which Slade were known for. While the soundtrack to *Slade in Flame* was a chart hit in England, the film itself was greeted with mixed reviews from critics and confusion from fans, and the band's popularity began to sharply decline not long after, something which the members at least partly attributed to the failure of the movie, though it has deservedly become much more widely appreciated in the ensuing years.

One of the most unique rock fantasy films of the '70s would have to be Brian De Palma's *Phantom of the Paradise* (1974), which put a unique spin of the familiar *Phantom of the Opera* tale. American composer, singer and actor Paul Williams, with his distinctive short stature and long blonde hair, composed the music and also stars in *Phantom of the Paradise* as Swan, a music producer who steals songs from singer-songwriter Winslow Leach (William Finley), and plans to use them to open up his prestige new concert hall The Paradise. When Leach becomes disfigured after falling into a record press while attempting to destroy copies of his music made without his permission or credit, he dons an owl-like silver mask and a black cape and begins to haunt and terrorise The Paradise and the acts that agree to perform there, while also trying to save pretty and talented, but naïve, young singer Phoenix (Jessica Harper). A Faustian tale filled with clever parody, a beautifully gaudy production design and colour palette, and a soundtrack that pays homage to multiple genres of pop and rock (from doo-wop and surf to pop and glam rock), *Phantom of the Paradise* remains one of De Palma's most vibrant and satisfying films. Sadly, the film was a commercial disappointment at first, though its score earned Oscar and Golden Globe nominations (Paul Williams also provided the singing voice for the

Phantom in the movie and on the soundtrack album), and its subsequent appreciation and lasting influence on later filmmakers and music video directors is clear.

The legendary English act the Who were a band that, given their creative penchant for recording thematic, rock opera concept albums, were a natural choice to have their music adapted to the screen. Their landmark 1969 album *Tommy*, about a "deaf, dumb, and blind kid" who "sure plays a mean pinball", was adapted into a superb satirical fantasy musical drama in 1975 by writer-director Ken Russell. Who frontman Roger Daltry played the charismatic title character, while the rest of the cast was divided between musicians (Elton John, Tina Turner, Eric Clapton, and Keith Moon) and legitimate actors (Ann-Margret, Oliver Reed, Jack Nicholson, and Robert Powell). Under Russell's guidance and unique sensibilities, *Tommy* became a hallucinogenic assault on the senses, and a masterclass in intelligent pop art presentation. Another Who concept album, 1973's *Quadrophenia*, which centred around the mod movement in London and Brighton in the mid '60, was also adapted for film in 1979, by director Franc Roddam (who would later go on to create the influential reality cooking show *Master Chef*!). Though it featured musicians like Toyah and Sting amongst its cast, *Quadrophenia* was a straight drama rather than a theatrical rock musical, though the soundtrack obviously uses a lot of the Who's music from the original album, along with

tracks by James Brown, The Ronettes, The Kingsmen and several others.

Not surprisingly, a number of '70s rock musical movies came from a theatrical source. *Jesus Christ, Superstar* (1973) and *Hair* (1979) were adapted from seminal stage musicals that were first produced during America's counterculture period, and were highly reflective of that era in both their music and approach. But the two big iconic pop-rock musicals of the decade were undoubtably *The Rocky Horror Picture Show* (1976) and *Grease* (1978). The former was adapted from the 1973 stage musical written by Richard O'Brien, and was a gloriously kinky love letter to classic Universal monster movies and B-grade science-fiction movies of the '50s, anchored by a career-defining performance by Tim Curry as the cross-dressing mad scientist from another planet, Dr. Frank N. Furter, and with a breakout role from Susan Sarandon as the innocent Janet Weiss. Like a lot of cult movies, *The Rocky Horror Picture Show* was initially a box-office flop, until it started attracting huge audiences to regular midnight screenings, where viewers would often dress up and recite out loud their favourite pieces of dialogue as they occurred in the movie. As the film became more well-known, the soundtrack also picked up steam, and one of the songs taken from it, the catchy *Time Warp*, reached no. 3 on the Australian singles charts, four years after the film's release.

Conversely, *Grease* became a box-office phenomenon right out of the gate, coming when it did at a time when its male lead, John Travolta, was just about the hottest name in entertainment, thanks to his starring role in *Saturday Night Fever* (1977) and the *Welcome Back, Kotter* television sit-com. The squeaky clean British-Australian singer Olivia Newton-John was also on the rise in the US, and when she and Travolta came together onscreen - playing high school students discovering both

love and themselves in the America of 1958 - the chemistry was palpable and undeniable, the pair forming one of cinema's most memorable couples. With original songs by Jim Jacobs and Warren Casey that celebrated the sounds and styles of early rock and roll, the initial stage production of *Grease*, which debuted in Chicago in 1971, was raunchier and a lot more risqué than Allan Carr's film adaptation, which was directed by Randall Kleiser. However, despite its lighter tone, the film still tackled some serious themes and subjects, including teen sex and the fear of pregnancy, peer and social pressures, and the gang violence which often erupted between different cliques of "greasers" (the hot-rod loving, leather-jacket wearing, greasy-haired boys from which the movie takes its title). Though it was originally produced for television as an NBC movie of the week (appropriately debuting on Halloween weekend), *KISS Meets the Phantom of the Park* was released theatrically in many other countries, where it was retitled *Attack of the Phantoms* (and simply as *KISS Phantoms*

in Italy). Directed by Gordon Hessler and also starring Anthony Zerbe, the Hanna-Barbera production depicted KISS as rock and roll superheros, who find themselves battling robotic

clones of themselves when they perform a string of concerts at the famous Magic Mountain amusement park in California. Along with its new title, *Attack of the Phantoms* was also reedited somewhat, to make it flow a bit more smoothly as a theatrical feature (TV movies were usually edited with regular commercial breaks in mind). The original incidental music, composed by Hoyt Curtain, was also largely removed, and replaced with a selection of songs from the four KISS solo albums, which had been released a year earlier amidst much hype but disappointing sales. Combined, actual sales of the KISS solo albums were around 1.5 million, certainly a very respectable figure, but the band's label, Casablanca Records, had pressed and shipped over one million copies of each album, resulting in a flood of unsold records being returned. By editing some of the solo songs into *Attack of the Phantoms*, it was hoped it might help stimulate sales of the four albums in international markets, especially in Australia where the band's popularity had skyrocketed by 1979. While *KISS Meets the Phantom of the Park/Attack of the Phantoms* is now considered a camp cult classic of sorts, and embraced by many KISS fans, at the time it was considered something of an embarrassment, which further alienated the older fans and emphasised the band's increasing appeal towards younger kids.

Inspired by The Beatles groundbreaking 1967 album, *Sgt.*

Pepper's Lonely Hearts Club Band (1978) was a much-hyped Robert Stigwood jukebox musical that, considering its source material and the appearance by '70s superstars Peter Frampton and The Bee Gees, should have been an easy hit. Instead, it was sadly disappointing in just about every aspect, and downright terrible and embarrassing in many. Today it remains largely forgotten, and the popularity of its two main acts certainly suffered in the wake of its critical lambasting and tepid commercial reception. The only bright spot for the film was its soundtrack, which featured covers of Beatles songs from Frampton and the Bee Gees as well as acts like Aerosmith, Earth, Wind & Fire, Alice Cooper, and managed to go platinum in America.

Another television movie which is worth mentioning is *Cotton Candy* (1978), which debuted on NBC only two nights before *KISS Meets the Phantom of the Park*. Only the second feature to be directed by young *Happy Days* star Ron Howard (his first being 1977's *Grand Theft Auto*), *Cotton Candy* tells the tale of a bunch of high school misfits (led by Charles Martin Smith and Ron's brilliant character actor brother Clint) who decide to form their own rock group in order to compete in a local Battle of the Bands contest, where they need to beat fellow high school heavyweights Rapid Fire, an obnoxious group of flashy KISS/Van

Halen-esque wannabees.

Co-written by Ron and Clint (who also authored a paperback tie-in for the movie), *Cotton Candy* turned up regularly on late late-night Melbourne TV in the mid '80s and became required viewing for a bunch of my stoner friends and I whenever it aired. Most of the film was shot in Texas at Lake Highlands High School and the Town East Mall in Mesquite. Unfortunately, it has never been released except by bootleg dealers in pretty inferior quality prints, and you can also find it on You Tube, but apparently Ron Howard himself does not want the movie being seen, which is unfortunate as it is far more entertaining than many of his later bloated Hollywood productions.

Directed by Allan Arkush for Roger Corman's New World Pictures, *Rock 'n' Roll High School* (1979) managed to succeed in the two main areas where the likes of *KISS Meets the Phantom of the Park* and *Sgt. Pepper's*

Lonely Hearts Club Band failed, in that it delivered a fun and entertaining story in its own right, while also being able to really capture the spirit of the band that it was showcasing. In this case, it was the New York punk rock group the Ramones. While now considered highly important and influential (in 2002, 'Spin' magazine ranked them only second to The Beatles as the greatest band of all time), in 1979 the Ramones were much more of a cult band in terms of their audience, making them something of a surprising choice at the time to have a film developed around them. Actually, it was not so much a surprising choice as it was a perfect one, since Roger Corman was never going to afford a KISS or an Aerosmith, he had to look at acts who were bubbling under the surface and would be more attainable. Reportedly, Cheap Trick and Tom Petty and the Heartbreakers were amongst the acts considered before the Ramones were decided upon.

Initially, *Rock 'n' Roll High School* was written as *Disco High*, and planned to take advantage of the disco craze that followed *Saturday Night Fever* (1977). But by the time the film was given the go-ahead, disco was already falling out of favour with many record buyers, so the decision was made to shift the focus from disco to the perennially popular rock genre. Set in the fictional Vince Lombardi High School (it was actually filmed at the recently-closed Mount Carmel High School in Los Angeles), P. J. Soles plays Riff Randall, the biggest Ramones fanatic at the school, but also its most troublesome student, constantly incurring the wrath of Principal Evelyn Togar (the great Mary Woronov). When Togar confiscates Riff's prized ticket to the upcoming Ramones concert, she has to rely on winning a radio contest in order to get to see her idols play, and hopefully get the chance to give them the lyrics to a song she has written for them (the titular "Rock 'n' Roll High School"). The film climaxes with Togar attempting to hold a rock music record burning in the school yard, until the students (with the Ramones in tow) overthrow the teachers and take command of the school, ultimately burning it down in a final act of fiery rebellion.

Rock 'n' Roll High School works so well because it doesn't ask the Ramones to do anything but be themselves, has a terrific soundtrack, and is filled with an assortment of memorable characters brought to life by a great cast of supporting actors which, apart from Woronov, also includes Clint Howard, Paul Bartel, Dick Miller, and Vince Van Pattern. And it's really nice to see the very appealing P. J. Soles get a well-deserved starring role in a film, after impressive turns in *Carrie* (1976) and *Halloween* (1978).

Rock 'n' Roll High School opened to fair box-office (considering its relatively low budget of $200,000) and quickly became something of a cult film, especially amongst punk fans. While *Road to Ruin* (1978), the band's most recent studio album prior to the movie being released, did not even crack the Billboard top hundred, their subsequent recording, *End of the Century* (1980), became their highest-charting album in America, peaking at No. 44, indicating that *Rock 'n' Roll High School* had some sort of effect on their popularity (or at least, did nothing to adversely affect it, like the KISS movie did). Released just a few months before the start of a new decade, it provided a fitting bridge between the rock and punk '70s and the new wave '80s that were beckoning.

Caricatures by Aaron Stielstra

Michael Beck in *The Warriors* (pg. 67)

David Patrick Kelly *in The Warriors* (pg. 67)

Vincent Schiavelli in *Taking Off* (pg. 78)

Gene Hackman in *Scarecrow* (pg. 54)

Alida Valli in *Lisa and the Devil* (pg. 38)

CLIMB ABOARD THE AVALANCHE EXPRESS

by Kevin Nickelson

"It was the first time I'd ever done anything on this scale. It was a $12 million dollar picture. I had $3 million that I was spending myself"- uncredited co-director Monte Hellman (from the book 'Monte Hellman: His Life and Films' by Brad Stevens).

Leslie Halliwell used to refer to any film script that exemplified a long-standing formula, especially in action-adventures and thrillers, as "thick ear material". For *Avalanche Express* (1979), that wording serves dually to describe both the story and the physical features of its aging star cast. Headlining old hands include Lee Marvin, Linda Evans, Robert Shaw, Maximilian Schell and Mike Connors, all lending their talents to the story of a defecting enemy spy needing protection and rescue. Under the keen eye and guidance of Mark Robson - a director well-heeled in such fare (the superb, underrated 1963 gem *The Prize* with Paul Newman and Elke Sommer might be his best entry in the genre) - such a project should have been a smooth road to travel. Except in Tinseltown, the ride always hits a pothole!

The film is based on a 1976 novel by Raymond Harold Sawkins, who often used the pseudonym Colin Forbes for his espionage-themed thrillers. He was remained active from the late '60s until his death in 2006. The plot depicts a Soviet General named Marenkov (Shaw) deciding to switch allegiance to the West, prompting the CIA to send top agent Harry Wargrave (Marvin) and his team to get him out. Wargrave decides to use the assignment to flush out as many KGB covert agents as he can in the European network by staging the defection publicly on a

fictional train called the Atlantic Express. KGB chief Bunin (Schell) takes the bait, sending every killer at his disposal to foil Harry and his friends. It is Bunin who deliberately starts the titular avalanche in a desperate attempt to stop Marenkov's defection.

What results is an exciting mashup of gunplay, explosions and edge-of-the-seat moments. Simultaneously, the events transpiring behind the scenes were to prove just as intriguing as anything taking place on screen.

After principal shooting in Ireland had been completed, and post-production had begun, both director Robson and co-star Shaw passed away suddenly (in June and August 1978, respectively). Lorimar Productions found themselves with quite a headache after Robson's death, as he'd only completed a rough cut of the work. The studio brought in Monte Hellman to finish directing, while Gene Corman (Roger's brother) was hired to take over Robson's producing duties.

Hellman discussed many of the problems he faced in Brad Stevens' book 'Monte Hellman: His Life and Films'. "There was already a rough cut of Robson's material when I came on board. Robson's editor, Dorothy Spencer, had edited '70s films, including some of my favorites like *Stagecoach*, *To Be or Not to Be* and *My Darling Clementine*. Without blaming her, she was not able in her initial attempt to make a coherent and dramatic cut of the material she had to work with. I felt I had to replace her, not because I didn't feel she was capable of performing her job, but because I felt she was so loyal to her former boss that she wouldn't be able to accept the kinds of changes that I felt were needed to make a passably acceptable movie.

I'd hired Garth Craven, who I'd met on *The Killer Elite,* to replace her. We threw out everything Dorothy had done and started from scratch."

Hellman also brought in writer Rospo Pallenberg, to revise the original script by Abraham Polonsky. Pallenberg was instructed to work what had been shot already and what was still to be shot into his script. "Much of what we hoped to shoot, including action scenes to be shot in Europe, was cancelled for budgetary reasons," explained

Hellman. "I was sent to Munich to research some of these scenes. Originally, I had been hired as producer/director. It was decided to bring in Gene Corman as producer, and I would be confined to just directing. From this point on, the process became very political. I had to fight for all my ideas, usually sending a memo each day to Peter Bart, then head of production at Lorimar, with copies to about twenty other people. Incidentally, real-life Soviet defector Anatoly Davidov was hired as translator for the new opening sequence done in Russian with accompanying English subtitles."

Shaw's untimely passing in August 1978 added more obstacles for the auteur. Looping the dialogue was particularly tricky without Shaw, though there was one accidental side-benefit. "Davidov co-directed the looping with Max Schell and Robert Rietty (who I hired to revoice Shaw)," said Hellman. "All of Shaw's dialogue throughout the film was replaced by Rietty. To keep consistent sound quality, all Max Schell's dialogue was looped, as was much of Lee Marvin's. One of the side-benefits with Schell was eliminating some of his German accent, which had been distracting in his original dialogue. The side-benefit of Rietty doing Shaw was eliminating Shaw's Scottish accent, which was hard to explain in a Russian!"

The action set-piece at the core of this tale, a gigantic avalanche intentionally triggered to destroy the train, was handled chiefly by Hellman. A few Robson-helmed interior reaction scenes were inserted. Hellman also shot the scene prior, in which the Davos Institute helicopter surveys the mountain pass. The whole sequence was no easy task to finish. Hellman commented: "I did some terrific matte work, traveling mattes. I shot anything connected to the avalanche, including all the people in the town, at the tavern, etc. I did an avalanche that wipes out a village and wipes out all the people in the foreground. It was a 70mm matte shot. Each take cost $100,000, and we did two takes and failed. I convinced them to let me try one more time and we got it. And that was a great joy."

He used miniatures for the external train shots (even the opening sequence) and shot the helicopter interiors on soundstages with process backgrounds. All interiors were shot in L.A., mostly on the Warner lot, though part of the big matte shot was done at Universal and part of the same scene was done at Paramount. He was also involved in a lot of new material for the boat battle just before the end, though it was officially directed by stunt director Alan Gibbs. The sequence was part of the new script Hellman had asked Pallenberg to create. "I did a lot of the planning, location scouting, etc., because I thought I was going to direct it," he explained. "Then the powers that be decided to use a stunt coordinator!"

Of the cast, Hellman seemed to have fond memories of working with the rugged Marvin. Sadly, he did not get to

LAWINEN EXPRESS

work with Shaw. "I enjoyed Lee (Marvin) tremendously. I was told to beware of his drinking problem, but I didn't find him hard to work with in any way." All the footage featuring Shaw during the final scenes was taken completely from what Robson had filmed. "Shaw was not on the set at the end - it was merely an identical set, which we tried to match to the original. There was a shot of Robert Shaw in the end, but I don't think it was a complete scene."

What stands out, truly, are the gorgeous locations used to frame the story. The Piazza della Scala and La Scala Opera House in Milan, Italy look glorious. Many of the exteriors were done in beautiful County Dublin in Ireland. A few moments were lensed in ever-photogenic London. The visual effort gives a true professional gloss to this globe-trotting spy melodrama. Coming in with a budget of $12 million, the picture went out on US domestic release on October 19th, 1979, to very mixed reviews and disappointing box office.

Vincent Canby of the 'New York Times', wrote a review for the October 19th edition, saying: "As junk movie melodramas go, *Avalanche Express* is of a not-quite-all-star tackiness that should make Sir Lew Grade furious with envy. Indeed, though the Abe Polonsky screenplay is based on a novel by Colin Forbes, the story about United States and Soviet agents, set mostly aboard a European train,

seems to have been lifted from Sir Lew's *The Cassandra Crossing*, but why anyone would want it is difficult to fathom." Canby would add, with tongue firmly in cheek: "*Avalanche Express* hasn't any wit but it has a few laughs, such as the sight of Joe Namath reacting when one actor delivers some startling information to another actor. Apparently told to do something, Joe looks hurt and surprised, as if no one wanted his autograph. The other actors are also at a loss."

In an intriguing sidenote, though Hellman and Corman do not receive official credit on-screen as co-director and co-producer respectively, they do get a mention in the acknowledgments section. "The producers wish to express their appreciation to Monte Hellman and Gene Corman for their post-production services."

Hellman used his rescue job on *Avalanche Express* to his advantage. When he went to Cannes in May 1979, shortly after completing *Avalanche Express* and getting Lorimar out of a deeply problematic hole, he took opportunity to sell his western *China 9, Liberty 37* to the company. He'd done them a huge favour and he fully intended to call it in. "This was the only deal I actually made at a festival. I literally hid the only videotape from my competition - who were trying to sell a badly cut Italian version to a schlock distributor - until I could close the deal with Lorimar," he remarked. Apparently, government spies aren't the only ones skilled in sneak tactics!

As for *Avalanche Express* itself, it's a lush-looking and suspenseful spy thriller, well worth a look. Ignore the naysayers and give it a shot.

Freewheelin' Again
SCARECROW

by Dr. Andrew C. Webber

Gene Hackman was a surprisingly big (and busy) star of '70s cinema, leaving his mark on a number of big hits (*The Poseidon Adventure, The French Connection* and *Superman*, etc.) but also choosing lesser movies which have matured with time (*Prime Cut, The Conversation* and *Night Moves,* for example). He was also one of the many stars who signed on for Richard Attenborough's fabulous war film *A Bridge Too Far* (1977), a candidate for the most impressively cast film the period, surely. The great thing about Hackman was that regardless of the film he appeared in, he was always watchable.

Al Pacino was at the time one of the new generation of '70s actors who firmly established himself in the early part of the decade, notably, of course, in T*he Godfather* films, but he was (dare I say) even better in Sidney Lumet's *Dog Day Afternoon* (1975). Pacino (a product of New York's Actors Studio) had made his film debut in *The Panic in Needle Park* (1971), an early example of the drug drama genre, which was directed by Jerry Schatzberg, a former

photographer for 'Vogue' who also, interestingly, found one of his images being used by Bob Dylan on his iconic *Blonde on Blonde* album cover.

Schatzberg is another of those minor American filmmakers (rather like Stuart Rosenberg and Michael Ritchie) whose work in the '70s is slightly under-rated. He made, for example, the Faye Dunaway fashion model expose *Puzzle of a Downfall Child* in 1970 (and went on to become Ms Dunaway's fiancé - though they never married); Alan Alda's political satire *The Seduction of Joe Tynan* in 1979 (which also features an early performance from Meryl Streep, when she was ethereal and angelic, and *Nashville's* Barbara Harris), and ended the decade with *Honeysuckle Rose*, one of the many late '70s early '80s movies with a focus on the downside of the American music business. *Honeysuckle Rose* starred the none-more-'70s Dyan Cannon (who also made an impact in Lumet's *The Anderson Tapes* in 1971 and Beatty's *Heaven Can Wait* in 1978) and country-and-western legend Willie

Nelson (who had made his film debut in Sydney Pollack's *The Electric Horseman* in 1979 and would be used to great effect by Michael Mann in his brilliant debut *Thief/Violent Streets* a few years later).

In 1973 Schatzberg, Hackman and Pacino (who, in the same year, starred in the hugely successful Sidney Lumet true-life cop drama *Serpico*) teamed up for the road movie *Scarecrow*, an apparently unhappy shoot, both Hackman and Pacino adopting very different approaches to acting which caused some friction on set.

This was one of those early '70s movies (like Monte Hellman's *Two-Lane Blacktop*, Peter Fonda's *The Hired Hand* and Dennis Hopper's *The Last Movie*) which took advantage of the new open door policy in Hollywood to the guys with long hair and beards. It proved another of those films which, unlike *Easy Rider*, failed to make much impact at the box office.

Arguably by 1973 Warner Brothers should have known better - but both Hackman and Pacino had proved themselves bankable stars. Schatzberg had a reasonable track record and the film's budget was presumably pretty low, apparently the main reason it got made.

Behind the camera was the mighty Vilmos Zsigmond, who had also shot both of Robert Altman's revisionist masterpieces *McCabe and Mrs Miller* (1971) and *The Long Goodbye* (1973) plus John Boorman's *Deliverance* (1972). Over the next few years, he would go on to apply his eye to films by, amongst others, Brian De Palma, Steven Spielberg and Michael Cimino (he shot both *The Deer Hunter* in 1978 and the notorious disaster *Heaven's Gate* (which has, of course, gone on to acquire the status of one of the greatest of all westerns and is a contender, alongside Malick's 1976 *Days of Heaven*, for one of the most beautiful films ever made).

It was written by Garry Michael White, whose only other credit of note was *Sky Riders,* the James Coburn hang-gliding heist movie (yup, you read that right) in 1976. The editing was by Evan A Lottman, who would be nominated for an Oscar for his work on *The Exorcist* a year later. The soundtrack was composed by Fred Myrow, who also scored Richard Fleischer's cult science fiction drama *Soylent Green* the following year (Fleischer another of those interesting '70s directors well deserving a 'Cinema of the '70s' re-appraisal - *The Last Run* from 1971 is especially good and his 1975 *Mandingo* has its admirers).

Essentially, *Scarecrow* is a two-handed road movie in which a mis-matched pair of drifters drift (what a surprise) across America, pursuing Hackman's dream of starting up a car wash in Pittsburgh. Along the way, the usual rather aimless encounters we expect from the genre take place; the buddies fall out and make up and there's a small role for Eileen Brennan, who had previously featured in Bogdanovich's *The Last Picture Show* (1971) and would later appear alongside Redford and Newman in *The Sting* (1973), Burt Reynolds in *Hustle* (1975) and Peter Falk in *The Cheap Detective* (1976).

Scarecrow shared the Cannes Film Festival interim Palme d'Or prize with Alan Bridges' *The Hireling* in the year of its release but died a death at the box office and reviews were mediocre, with Stanley Kauffmann claiming that the film was "a picture that manages to abuse two American myths at once - the Road and the Male Pair." Ouch!

This didn't halt the "freewheelin' tide," however, and, in 1974 audiences went on to experience, amongst others, the adventures of similarly mis-matched buddies in Altman's *California Split* (Segal and Gould), Mazursky's *Harry and Tonto* (Art Carney and, well, a cat), Rush's *Freebie and the Bean* (with added auto-destruction plus Caan and Arkin) and Cimino's *Thunderbolt and Lightfoot* featuring Clint Eastwood and an impossibly young Jeff Bridges (although by 1975, apart from Altman's "ultimate" freewheeler *Nashville,* it was almost all over bar the shouting - Dick Richards' *Rafferty and the Gold Dust Twins* and Frank Perry's *Rancho Notorious* arguably the only other notable films that year

with a similar 'loose' road movie vibe). Maybe the times they were a changin', as the man said and '70s audiences were increasingly used to TV's more formulaic approach to narrative? Or, perhaps the new blockbusters like *The Towering Inferno* (1974), *Jaws* (1975) and *King Kong* (1976) meant that spectators began expecting a movie experience every time they visited the cinema —rather than something a little more rambling and slight?

And that's exactly how you'd describe *Scarecrow* - but in a good way. It rambles and it's slight but, by the end, you've begun to care about the protagonists and even though it wasn't exactly a rollercoaster, you've enjoyed the ride. It's the same feeling you get at the end of Stuart Rosenberg's *Pocket Money,* for example, or maybe a Raymond Carver short story. Essentially, it's a *Midnight Cowboy*-style story of two drifters (Max and 'The Lion' played respectively by Hackman and Pacino), their shared dream of opening a car wash in Pittsburgh and the problems that befall them on the journey to get there.

It's all beautifully shot (as you'd imagine), surprisingly brutal (especially a sexual assault by the repellent Richard Lynch as prison trustee Reilly on Pacino's character whilst the pair stop-over in a small prison following a bar-room brawl in Denver which is accompanied by Carole King's *You Make Me Feel Like a Natural Woman* on the jukebox) and very much "of its time" (Hackman's character is irresistible to women for some reason, most notably Brennan's surprisingly feisty tramp and Ann Wedgworth, who plays his former partner's partner Frenchie - "Where did

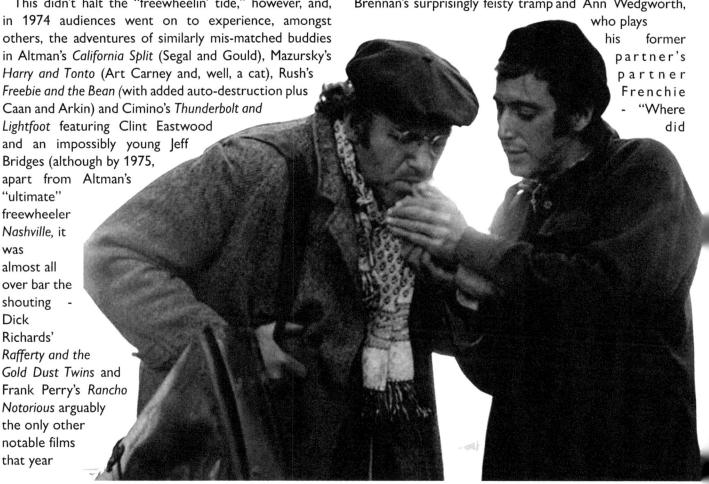

you get that name from?" asks Max, lasciviously).

Like so many great '70s movies, it ends bleakly with Pacino losing it in the middle of a beautiful fountain in the heart of Detroit after his ex-wife (falsely) reveals to him the fact that the child he thought they had together had died and then makes up for this with a final image of Hackman banging his shoe heel on the desk of a bemused airport saleswoman as he finally gets to buy his ticket to dreamland.

In the end, it's hard to see quite where the film is going with its central symbol of the scarecrow being effective because it makes crows laugh - rather than scare them off. And it's very odd (especially after *The Godfather*) to see Pacino hamming it up with a series of goofy impersonations and oddball gags (although, after seeing him in the dreadful *House of Gucci* recently, I guess we shouldn't really have expected anything else). But, in spite of its quirks (and occasional longueurs), *Scarecrow* is definitely an interesting, if minor, addition to the stream of freewheelin' road movies which were released in the early '70s.

"John D Rockefeller, JP Morgan, Andrew Carnegie. Max and Lion" ran the movie's ironic "American dream is bust" tagline. It could just have equally read: *"Five Easy Pieces, Emperor of the North, The Last Detail. Scarecrow."*

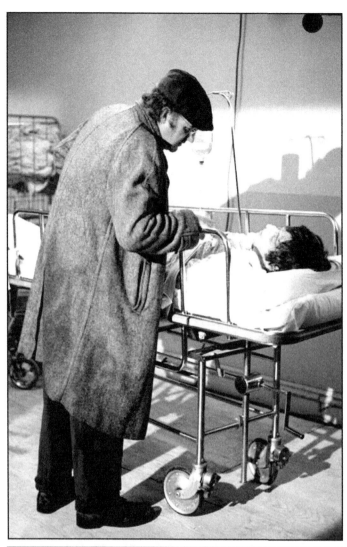

Game Match Point

XY&Zee

by Rachel Bellwoar

When is a game of ping-pong more than a game of ping-pong? When it takes place over the opening titles of Brian G. Hutton's *X, Y and Zee* (1973). Sure, Zee (Elizabeth Taylor) and her husband Robert (Michael Caine) look happy enough. The match doesn't appear particularly heated but it's still a competition. Hints of the volatile nature of their marriage can still be identified within the outwardly syrupy scene.

Too happy can be just as suspicious as too angry, and thanks to the decision to have an instrumental version of Ted Myers and Jaiananda's song *Going in Circles* playing over the game (which in the beginning is filmed in slow-mo, for an even more "aw shucks" quality), they seem almost obnoxiously happy together - a couple who truly get along and enjoys each other's company.

Later the film will end with the same song playing but with the lyrics sung by Three Dog Night, and the words completely change the nature of the song. Suddenly, instead of coming across as cheery, the tune becomes a lament for this unhealthy couple who won't change and continue to make the same mistakes over and over again. That this song bookends the movie tells you everything you need to know about their relationship - the song stays the same because it still applies to their marriage. The only thing that changes is they bring another person down with them and that person is Stella, played by Susannah York.

Stella isn't in the opening titles, but her role in the movie as "the other woman" is already telegraphed by the placement of her name. Whereas the camera turns to Taylor and Caine during their respective credits, when York's name pops up the visual is of a blue backdrop and the ping-pong ball moving back and forth across the screen. The suggestion, of course, is that Stella is going to come between Zee and Robert and, essentially, she does. But what's odd about *X, Y and Zee* is that while Stella is technically the other woman, it's Zee who gets treated like the third wheel most of the time. She's the one who is being wronged, yet somehow she's the nuisance. It's like a gaslighting movie without a catharsis moment at the end wherein everyone realizes Zee wasn't as crazy as her husband liked to make out.

The casting of Elizabeth Taylor also feels very intentional, in terms of making Zee someone who could never be the wronged party because how could someone with such a big personality be vulnerable? Taylor's own strength and marital history is used to make the character culpable. Just because Zee doesn't break down, responding to her husband's philandering by fighting back, somehow means she forfeits the right to be upset - it makes her anger is naggy instead of justified. *Fatal Attraction* is what affairs are supposed to look like. In that film, the other woman is the person acting the most erratic so it's easy to blame her when things go wrong. Zee is Robert's wife, yet *X, Y and Zee* still tries to blame her purely because she doesn't take Robert's cheating lying down.

That isn't to say Zee's an innocent party, because she's definitely not. Zee never misses an opportunity to get a rise out of her husband, and that means stooping to new lows to get his attention, but (just as he does in the ping-pong game during the opening titles) Robert matches her point for point. He's the one who initiates the affair and he's the one who never expresses regret.

He does say one thing that could be construed as regret. During their first date Robert tells Stella: "I wish we had met in a different place." A simple enough statement, but one that's hard to believe given how their first meeting actually goes down, with them meeting at a party where Zee is there to witness them together. Had they met somewhere else, there might've been a window where Zee didn't know about the affair.

If secrecy was really important to Robert, he would've never gone about his courtship of Stella so publicly. Meeting someone and falling for them is one thing, but Robert asks to be introduced. He immediately involves his and Zee's mutual friends. His intentions are extremely obvious from the start and he doesn't make any effort to hide them. Usually there's at least one party concerned about scandal, but since neither Zee nor Robert seem to care what anyone thinks, *X, Y and Zee* is a film without brakes. At times, this allows this film to be honest and brutal. It also can leave the characters stuck, especially when the only one who goes through any sort of transformation is meant to be the villain at the end of the day.

Zee and Robert's marriage is an abusive one, but Zee genuinely wants to save it. From the moment Stella appears on screen, she and Zee are pitted against each other, with the comparison meant to flatter Stella and condemn Zee. Starting with appearances, the

very first fight on-screen fight Zee and Robert have is over what Robert should wear to the party. Zee wants him to wear something colorful, but Robert opts for a formal shirt. Meanwhile, the first thing Robert notices about Stella at the party is that she's wearing a silver dress (it's what he uses to identify her when he's trying to find out more about her). Without anything else to go on, Robert falls for Stella because she's the opposite of his wife - blonde instead of brunette, with more natural make-up (whereas Zee has on bold eye shadow and an orange frock).

Even the sound cues for Zee and Stella are meant to reflect their opposing temperaments. Whereas Stella becomes associated with wind chimes, Zee often enters a scene in conjunction with rock music, the better to paint her out as this loud and intrusive force. Far from being gentle, the transitions in this movie are aggressive, too, particularly when it goes from Stella and Robert's first date

to the honking of Zee in her red car, as she pulls up to Stella's store. The contrast is so sharp that it feels harsh, even though it's technically a dissolve. Another dissolve that feels like a slap in the face is when Robert and Zee appear to be having a truce. Zee certainly looks hopeful, but then the scene dissolves to show Robert and Stella in bed together, proving Robert's words to be completely hollow.

It all goes back to that opening ping-pong match, and Robert and Zee's insistence on pretending what they're doing is still a game and hasn't turned into something more destructive. When exactly that change happens is hard to pinpoint and probably isn't the same for both characters, since it takes Zee a lot longer to realize Stella is sticking around (even though on a subconscious level she must realize Stella's not a fling or she wouldn't lash out as much as she does). Taylor's physicality in the role is light and

60

breezy, too, like when Zee realizes she's accidentally crashed Robert and Stella's dinner plans and takes a moment to exercise before opening the door to let Stella in. It's a silly gesture that would suggest that their fighting's all in good fun, but games have rules and this one doesn't.

Robert is ultimately the film's biggest hypocrite. He gets angry whenever Zee even suggests having an affair, even though he's in the midst of a full-fledged one himself. Transparency is somehow supposed to make what he's doing OK. He doesn't hide that he's cheating, so somehow that's better than going behind Zee's back.

If Robert is the most deserving of criticism, some should be directed at Stella as well. While undoubtedly the film's one passive character, she's not naïve nor is she entirely a victim. While Zee is constantly called out whenever she's irritating or rattles on for too long, Stella (because she doesn't act out in public) is allowed to carry on with her delusions without any pushback. Mainly, Stella never seems to admit the part that she's playing in breaking up Zee and Robert's marriage. Her deniability comes from the fact that she never actually agrees to the arrangement but just seems to let the relationship happen. It's Robert who actively pursues her, to the point of getting physically aggressive (grabbing her necklace and not letting go when she moves to walk away). Especially during their early interactions it's hard to tell if Stella even likes Robert but while she might not respond to his advances in the moment, she still meets up with him again and frequently wears the same necklace he once used to control her in later scenes.

Zee is the only character who changes in *X, Y and Zee*. Her musical cue even changes to reflect how depressed she's become, but given the choice to go real or lurid, Edna O'Brien's screenplay chooses lurid every time and the sudden introduction of a lesbian relationship comes in too late to be anything of substance beyond provoking shock and evoking memories of York's performance in *The Killing of Sister George* (a film about an abusive relationship between two women).

X, Y and Zee may be trashy at its core, but it's trash in the best sense with a performance by Taylor that is up there with her other Grand Guignol roles in films like *Boom!* and *The Driver's Seat*.

THE DUELLISTS

"Even Giants Start Small"

by James Lecky

During the Napoleonic Wars, a vicious and bloody vendetta erupts between two French cavalry officers, Gabriel Feraud (Harvey Keitel) and Armand d'Hubert (Keith Carradine), leading to a series of duels which range over the next sixteen years, encompassing the rise, campaigns and ultimate defeat of Napoleon Bonaparte.

A quick precis of *The Duellists* does it little justice. Based upon 'The Duel' (also known as 'The Point of Honour'), a short story by Joseph Conrad first published in 1908, the slim storyline of both the film and the original encompass themes of honour, obsession, brutality and, ultimately, the futility of violence. This is a film of mood and tone, anchored by two superb central performances.

At first glance, both Keith Carradine and Harvey Keitel might seem improbable leads for a European period piece. Keitel had appeared in a trio of Scorsese movies - *Mean Streets* (1973), *Alice Doesn't Live Here Anymore* (1974), *Taxi Driver* (1976) - while Carradine had major supporting roles in Robert Aldrich's *Emperor of the North Pole* (1973), with Lee Marvin and Ernest Borgnine, and in Robert Altman's *Nashville* (1975) but neither men were international draws. It is probable that the film's American backers wanted at least a couple of U.S actors in the mix, if only to offset the predominantly British cast but, nevertheless, Carradine and Keitel are perfect in their roles, bringing a New World energy into an Old World story.

Keitel's Feraud is the hammer, determined to right an imagined wrong at any cost, whilst Carradine's d'Hubert is the anvil, equally as determined to hold onto his honour, but all too aware of how ridiculous and uncontrollable the

situation has become. At one point, the two men fight side by side during the disastrous 1812 campaign in Russia, saving each other's lives against marauding Cossacks, but even this is not enough to satisfy the honour-obsessed Feraud, and his refusal of a celebratory drink shows exactly how consumed by his singular vendetta he has become.

The Duellists is essentially a series of linked set pieces, with each of the duels serving to move the narrative on. Visually, its touchstone is Stanley Kubrick's elegant *Barry Lyndon* (1975), yet Scott also manages to reference his own work - the opening scene with a young geese herder guiding her flock through the French countryside has echoes of his 1973 'Boy on the Bike' advertisement for the Hovis bakery - and its emphasis on action as much as character undercuts its more arthouse sensibilities.

The film is often brutal in its depiction of violence - the vicious cellar brawl repudiates any notion that this is a swashbuckler even if it may bear some passing resemblance to such classic swordplay movies as *The Adventures of Robin Hood* (1938), *Scaramouche* (1952), *The Prisoner of Zenda* (1937, remade in 1952) or the glorious Gene Kelly star vehicle *The Three Musketeers* (1948).

The swashbuckler was one of the great mainstays of the Golden Age of Hollywood, adventure films that were colourful (even in black and white), fast-paced and exciting - stars included Douglas Fairbanks Jr, (*The Corsican Brothers*, 1941) Errol Flynn (*The Sea Hawk*, 1940) and, toward the end of its heyday, Stewart Granger (*The Prisoner of Zenda*, *Scaramouche*, 1952). So popular was the form that it spawned a number of comic variations including *The*

Princess and the Pirate (1944) starring Bob Hope and Virginia Mayo, *The Court Jester* (1956) starring Danny Kaye and that most swashbuckling of all villains, Basil Rathbone. The form emerged again in the 21st century with *Pirates of the Caribbean: The Curse of the Black Pearl* (2003) and its various law-of-diminishing-returns sequels. The swashbuckler would raise its head sporadically during the '70s - *The Adventures of Gerard* (1970), *Royal Flash* (1975), *The Three Musketeers* and its immediate sequel *The Four Musketeers* (1973 & 1974), *Swashbuckler* (1976) and the Peter Sellers vehicles *Ghost in the Noonday Sun* (1973), and *The Prisoner of Zenda* (1979), all of which are, to a greater or lesser degree, lighthearted takes on the genre.

But for all its finely choreographed swordplay, *The Duellists* is not a swashbuckler. It is too intense and violent for that - the sword-cuts are too deep to be shrugged off, they take time to heal, and the encounters between Feraud and d'Hubert are delayed by them as much as by the importance of Napoleon's campaigns.

In some ways, *The Duellists* is Ridley Scott's take on the cinematic western, at least in the same sense that Michael Reeves' *Witchfinder General* (1968) might be classified as variation on the form. Of course, in American and European westerns, the duel is often an end in itself, particularly between protagonist/hero and antagonist/villain, with one or the other triumphant. But *The Duellists* has no real triumph or, for that matter, real hero. Certainly, the film is skewed in favour of d'Hubert and he is the character with whom we most sympathise, while Feraud is kept almost at arm's length, and we are given few glimpses into his psyche (for example, the horseback duel where the flashbacks are all from d'Hubert's perspective) or the real reasons for his singular and murderous pursuit. By inference, d'Hubert represents the aristocracy and Feraud the underclasses who rose to prominence under Napoleon, but neither perspective is made clear - other than by the performances or occasional snippets of dialogue ("Don't expect decency from his kind") and is left to the audience to deduce.

Neither Carradine or Keitel attempt cod-European accents

- or for that matter try to mimic the distinctly British tones of their co-stars - and this helps to reinforce their status as outsiders within the rigid strata of the French military. Neither, for that matter, does narrator Stacy Keach whose distinctive tones serve to link the various 'chapters' (a directorial choice that was, apparently, driven as much by budgetary constraints as artistic choice) and the intermingling of various voices and for that matter, acting styles serve to elevate what might otherwise have been a fairly simple and straightforward tale of rivalry and revenge.

Equally importantly, Scott never allows the film to drift from its central narrative. Sub-plots are few and fleeting and there is little fat on the relatively short running time (roughly an hour and forty minutes as compared to *Barry Lyndon*'s three hours) and time and time again, Scott uses action rather than words to propel the story - following their horseback duel, the triumphant d'Hubert leaps his horse over a hay wagon, his exuberance and relief on display for all to see.

There is an old adage that "even giants start small" and *The Duellists* might be seen as Scott laying the cinematic foundations for such epics as *1492: Conquest of Paradise* (1992), *Gladiator* (2000), *Kingdom of Heaven* (2005), *The Last Duel* (2021) and perhaps even coming full circle with the upcoming *Napoleon* (2023) with its return to 19th century Europe.

Prior to his cinematic debut, Scott had worked in television and, more importantly, in advertising, notably for the aforementioned Hovis as well as Benson and Hedges (featuring the iconic comic talents of Terry-Thomas and

Eric Sykes), creating pieces that were more akin to ultra-short films - a trend which flowed through '70s television and cinema advertising, reaching its apotheosis with the Bond-esque Milk Tray ad and the Leonard Rossiter/Joan Collins pairing which promoted that most '70s of alcoholic beverages, Cinzano.

This is not to say that, budgetary restrictions notwithstanding, *The Duellists* is a small film. It moves through time and place from France to German to Russia and returning to France for its denouement in a chaotic post-Napoleon world. If the major battles of the period are mostly off-screen, it serves to focus the story on character rather than spectacle - yet there is always the sense that great events are happening, events which dwarf the petty rivalry between Feraud and d'Hubert but never distract them from it.

And while Keitel and Carradine anchor the film, they are surrounded by a wealth of British acting talent, often in telling cameos. Albert Finney appears as Joseph Fouche, Napoleon's Minister of Police (a part he agreed to at the urging of his then-girlfriend, Diana Quick, who plays d'Hubert's mistress), Edward Fox, as a Bonapartist agent, Tom Conti as d'Hubert's flute-playing friend Dr Jacquin, Robert Stephens in a brief but barnstorming performance as Brigadier-General Trelliard, and appearances from Alun Armstrong, Liz Smith and Pete Postlethwaite (in a blink and you'll miss it moment).

Finney had risen to prominence in the '60s, but had achieved huge global success as Hercule Poirot in *Murder On the Orient Express* (1974). Fox had recently played an icy assassin in another critical and financial success *The Day of the Jackal* (1973), while Stephens - primarily a much-respected theatre actor, once regarded as natural successor to Laurence Olivier - had appeared in Billy Wilder's *The Private Life of Sherlock Holmes* to great and deserved acclaim. It is a credit to Scott's vision and, equally as importantly, the screenplay by Gerald Vaughan-Hughes, that actors of such calibre were drawn to a low budget film with a first-time feature director.

Lensed by Frank Tidy - who's subsequent career would include *Dracula* (1979), *Sweet Liberty* (1986) and

Stop! Or My Mom Will Shoot (1992) amongst others - the film often has an autumnal look, as though the glories of the First Republic and First Empire were already doomed to fade. The top of the frame often features lowering clouds, and the mud and snowbound scenes of the disastrous retreat from Moscow in 1812 practically emanate coldness from the screen with their deep shadows and frigid palate.

The score by Howard Blake is often haunting and never strays in the cod-historical that was a feature of the classic swashbuckler, helping to underscore the essential realism of the film. Blake, best known for his score for *The Snowman* (1982), provides some of his finest work here. His music is a vital part of the film together with Terry

Rawlings' superb sound design .

But the two pillars that *The Duellists* stands on are its stunning visuals and ferocious lead performances.

Feraud is a cauldron of seething rage. We never fully learn where that rage comes from - though there are hints along the way - but its only outlet is through the sword. Whatever truama lies in his past, d'Hubert is its embodiment: "I believe you feed your spite on him," d'Hubert's mistress tells him, and his angry response is near enough an admission that her statement is true. But his anger is cold and controlled, his contempt for his opponents only released with a dismissive "La!" when he strikes a telling blow.

D'Hubert is equally angry, but his anger comes from a sense of confusion, unsure of how and why the feud emerged but equally as determined as Feraud to protect his honour. Friends and comrades urge each man to apologise and end the violence but without result.

Both Carradine and Keitel give tightly controlled performances and at times put themselves through some brutal physical punishment (Keitel was electrocuted at one point during the cellar duel). They also insisted upon using real, and very dangerous, sabres for several fights, brilliantly staged by William Hobbs whose other credits include John Bormann's extraordinary *Excalibur* (1981), HBO's *Game of Thrones* and Hammer's underrated classic *Captain Kronos: Vampire Hunter* (1974), where he plays the undead swordsman Lord Durward in a rare on-screen role. (Hobbs also has a brief appearance in *The Duellists*).

Significantly, the film was produced by David Puttnam, the doyen of British cinema, a man who produced quality at a time when UK screens were dominated by TV spinoffs and the particular variety of British sex comedy that included the Robin Askwith *Confessions* films and their many imitators. Puttnam was involved in a number of important British films, including *That'll Be The Day* (1973), *Stardust* (1974), *Lisztomania* (1975), *Chariots of Fire* (1981) and *Local Hero* (1983) amongst others.

Above all, however - regardless of its provenance, superb central and supporting performances - *The Duellists* belongs to Ridley Scott. It is a film of singular directorial vision, a vision that would be seen and seen again in many of his subsequent films. *Alien* (1979) and *Blade Runner* (1982), while far removed from *The Duellists* in terms of genre and location, owe a lot to his debut, being both being essentially intimate character studies set against an unfamiliar backdrop - whilst *Kingdom of Heaven* (2005) is perhaps Scott's finest blending of the intimate and the epic.

Ridley Scott's journey as a filmmaker began with *The Duellists*, and it has provided a template for his best work ever since. A film of rare passion and skill.

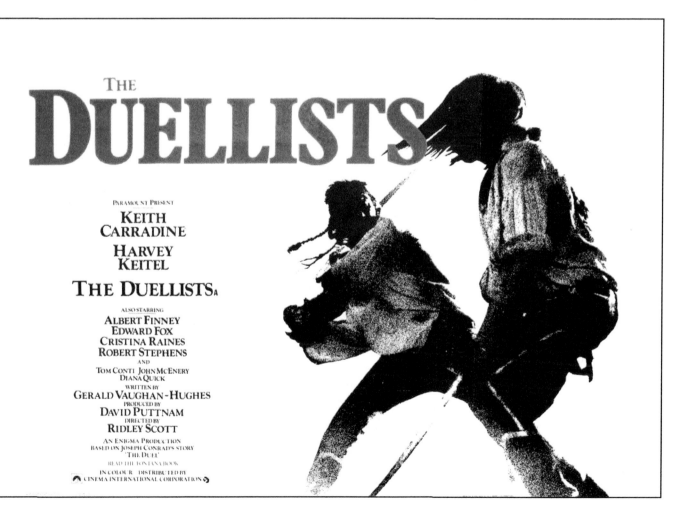

by Steven West

"Our film doesn't say everyone is supposed to be a lawyer of a doctor or something. The movie sees gangs as a defensive alignment in order to help you survive in a harsh atmosphere"
- Walter Hill, to the 'Village Voice' (2015).

The front page of the March 22nd 1972 issue of 'New York Magazine' promised a Student's Guide to Work and a thrilling article about the backstage battle over "No, No, Nanette"... but the immediate attention-grabber nodded to the controversy of *A Clockwork Orange*. "Are you ready for the new ultra-violence?" screamed the headline, accompanied by representations of four of the city's gangs - the Young Sinners, the Royal Javelins, the Black Assassins and the Reapers. The sub-heading, "The Return of the New York Street Gang" suggested this was nothing new, while the cover story by Gene Weingarten provided an analysis of gang origins, ethics and structures. The message, however, couldn't help but instil alarm: at least 70 street gangs in the Bronx alone, amounting to a gang population of around 4000. Weingarten closed on a portentous note, highlighting that those who thought this was just a repeated cycle in New York's history were fooling themselves: "The city has never before seen so much factory-made firepower in so many youthful, organised hands". Worse still, there's "no sensible, adequately financed plan equal to the threat".

Hollywood's 'New York Nightmare' films of the '70s fed on this kind of scaremongering, but Walter Hill's *The Warriors,* released at the tail end of the decade, took the opposite tack, with its origins in published works from an earlier decade and millennium. Hill, who sees all his films as

westerns and believes there are only two kinds of stories (the Odyssey and the Crucifixion), fashioned Sol Yurick's 1965 novel of the same name into a stylised, balletic urban western that had a bit of both. The harder-edged violence of Yurick's book was softened in the process and Hollywood studio concessions meant reworking the African American 'Warriors' of the novel into a mixed-race gang.

Lawrence Gordon had produced Hill's first two features as writer-director: the commercially and critically successful Charles Bronson vehicle *Hard Times* (1975) and the unloved, unprofitable *The Driver* (1978), dismissed by a pearl-clutching 'Los Angeles Times' reviewer as "ultra-violent trash" as if that were a bad thing. Gordon discovered Yurick's single night, July 4th-set novel in a bookstore and became fascinated by its basis in Greek history.

Yurick had encountered various so-called "juvenile delinquents" and youthful gang members while working as a social investigator for New York's welfare department in the '50s, amidst the rock 'n' roll era's moral panic. The empathetic and three-dimensional approach to *The Warriors'* characters reflects his experiences. His gang's quest to return home through rival gang territories mirrors the quest in Xenophon's seven-volume 'Anabasis', written around 370 B.C. and documenting the march of 10,000 Greek mercenaries as, following the death of their leader

Cyrus the Younger, they strive to overthrow his brother, King Artaxerxes II. The author and Hill took major narrative beats and names from Xenophon, including the plot catalyst of Cyrus' assassination in the first act, for which the Warriors are blamed.

For Hill, it was a larger-than-life piece with an inherent silliness - in his words it represented a "different kind of reality [and] only made sense as a comic book". The deployment of old-fashioned wipes, as alien to the New Hollywood decade as the '30s serial-style opening crawl of *Star Wars*, added to the intended artificiality. Hill's planned "Sometime in the future…" prologue would have illustrated the story's historical origins via comic panels and a voiceover by Orson Welles. The studio predictably hated the idea, fearing it would align it too closely to *Star Wars*, and it would eventually be seen (with Hill as narrator) in the slightly longer Director's Cut released in 2005.

Hill gave Bronson one of his finest screen roles in *Hard Times* and, on the surface, *The Warriors* visualises the worst lunatics-taking-over-the-asylum fears of his bereaved *Death Wish* character Paul Kersey. The Michael Winner film gleefully exploited early '70s New York crime statistics and paranoia for all they were worth, capturing a menacing (usually non-white) punk on every street corner. *The Warriors* unfolds in a hyper-real New York where the city's 20,000-strong police force is pitted against a potentially unified gang base of 60,000 "soldiers". The city no longer belongs to the conventional authorities, and the cops and fire chiefs are background figures in Hill's film, a far from positive, often disruptive force whose influence is waning. The film begins and ends at the Warriors' Coney Island home, the hopeful last scene confirming the script's success in offering a humanising, non-judgemental portrait of gang members.

The late Roger Hill had a rare film role as Cyrus, winning the part after the failure of initial plans to cast a real gang member (though hundreds of bona fide N.Y. gang members appear as extras). Cyrus, President of the largest gang, the Gramercy Riffs, organises a midnight meeting at Van Cortlandt Park, where nine delegates from each of the 100 gangs gather to a cry of "The future is ours". The plan to collectively take over the city one borough at a time falls apart with Cyrus' murder. The Warriors, themselves hosting internal tensions between James Remar's Ajax and Michael Beck's Swan, spend the film making their perilous way back to Coney Island. Prior to the 'New York Magazine' article, a similar number of city gangs gathered at the Bronx's Hoe Avenue Boys Club for an intended peace summit after the murder of Black Benji, an advocate for inter-gang peace from the "Ghetto Brothers".

The picture has a beautiful, vibrant young cast, some on their way to impressive careers. Detroit native David Patrick Kelly as Luther, the unhinged leader of the Rogues (and Cyrus' killer) was among those making his film debut, having portrayed another dangerous character, Charlie Blossom, in the Broadway musical *Working* which co-starred the versatile (and also, sadly, late) Lynne Thigpen. Her iconic role as the film's Greek chorus D.J. provides '70s cinema's most memorable lips after *The Rocky Horror Picture Show*. Hill and Gordon had seen

Working, the former liking Kelly's "Richard III quality" and casting him later in *48 Hrs* (1982) and *Last Man Standing* (1996), though he particularly excelled as Jerry Horne in *Twin Peaks* (1990-91/2017). He claimed to have based Luther's memorable chant of "Warriors come out to play-ay" on a neighbour who had robbed him. Beck, as the

Warriors' second-in-command, was cast on the strength of his role in Israeli film *Madman* (1978) and his co-star from that film, Sigourney Weaver, was considered for *The Warriors* before being cast in the Hill-produced *Alien* (1979). With Paramount nixing Hill's desire for a Puerto Rican actress as Mercy, girlfriend of Sully, leader of the Orphans, Deborah Van Valkenburgh got the role.

Cinematically, we're somewhere between a middle-class '70s New Yorker's ultimate nightmare and W*est Side Story*. Fight sequences involve switchblade-wielding roller-skaters and include a gloriously choreographed men's room battle-dance, unfolding like musical numbers and punctuated by Thigpen's sultry tones. Were it not for the various "fucks", this would have easily qualified for a 1979 PG-rating: the violence is seldom bloody or genuinely brutal. Great-looking, buff, bare-chested males resemble an urban boy band of some future decade as they engage in music video-like set pieces. Only occasionally does it veer into genuinely sinister territory, including Ajax's efforts to force himself on an undercover cop portrayed by future Oscar/Tony Award-winner Mercedes Ruehl in her first credited film role.

In the era of European synth pioneers like Tangerine Dream, Giorgio Moroder and Jean-Michel Jarre, it's all appropriately set to the beat of a marvellously insistent score by Barry De Vorzon. His work as a songwriter saw collaborations with artists like Marty Robbins and

The Cascades, while his film work has proven just as eclectic, ranging from original cues and arrangements for *Dillinger* (1973) and *Xanadu* (1980) to superb scores for William Peter Blatty's two directorial features, T*he Ninth Configuration* (1978) and *The Exorcist III* (1990). With The Eagles' revered guitarist Joe Walsh, he wrote the rousing track *In the City* bringing a dash of optimism to the closing scene. Generally afforded creative freedom, De Vorzon cannily created dropouts in his thrilling, driving main theme to accommodate pivotal early dialogue Hill required.

Multiple editors - including Woody Allen regular Susan E. Morse - worked simultaneously in three cutting rooms to get *The Warriors* into cinemas before other gangland pictures, notably Philip Kaufman's *The Wanderers*, released by Orion five months later. The postproduction frenzy is reflected in the punchy pacing, again aping the rhythm of a modern musical as it cuts between rival gangs and incorporates tooling-up montages.

Bobbie Manix, the costume designer who later worked

on *Xanadu* and Hill's *The Long Riders* (1980), was just as essential in giving the movie its unique ambience. In line with Hill, she took a fantasy approach to the multiple gangs' outfits, admitting that actual gangs would be unlikely to afford such ensembles. Inspired by the names and locations of the gangs, she separated them by colour, shape and fabric while traditional notions of gender-specific clothing were cast aside. Thus, we have the mime-like H-Hats, the female Lizzies with their transparent tops and trendy jackets, the baseball uniforms and painted faces of the Furies and the quilted satin appliques for the Riffs - all created from numerous pieces of clothing grabbed from scouring N.Y.C. outlets.

Hungarian cinematographer (and Holocaust survivor) Andrew Laszlo brought much innovation to the table. He had shot key early feature films for William Friedkin and Francis Ford Coppola and, appropriately enough, at New York's Shea Stadium, helped film, for The Beatles and producer Ed Sullivan, the first (14-camera) large-scale concert for U.S. television. Astutely using fluorescent subway lights, cheap drugstore lights clipped to trees and vivid primary colours reflected off perpetually wet surfaces, he gave it a gorgeously psychedelic look despite the challenges of the period's technology and the production's bold decision to forsake soundstages for real, neon/graffiti-drenched New York locations throughout. Laszlo would later work wonders with filters in swampland for Hill's *Southern Comfort* (1981) and low-light in Hill's full-blown "rock & roll" fable *Streets of Fire* (1984) - also starring Van Valkenburgh - while bringing an equally beguiling colour palette to Tobe Hooper's *The Funhouse* (1981), one of the best-looking U.S. horror films of its decade.

During a six-month period in which the box-office champs included *The Deer Hunter, The China Syndrome, Manhattan* and *Alien*, Paramount opened *The Warriors* on February 9th, 1979. It ended the long reign of Richard Donner's *Superman* at the top spot, albeit just for a fortnight. A commercial smash, it almost made back its reported $4 million budget within the first three days despite being largely met with critical brickbats. Not unusually, Pauline Kael got it, enthusing "The movie is like visual rock, and it's bursting with energy." Entirely expected, Siskel and Ebert got it completely wrong. Writing on February 13th, Ebert dismissed it as an "exercise in mannerism", criticising the things that make it so distinctive and thrilling: "plainly impossible" chase scenes and "People [moving] into their symbolic places with such perfectly timed choreography that they must be telepathic".

Controversy almost immediately followed. The 'New York Times' journalist Robin Herman, reporting on a series of violent incidents in theatres screening the film, also noted the "artful studied poses" of the characters while making the onscreen violence sound much more brutal than it is, citing "a head-cracking brawl in a subway bathroom with weapons ranging from knives and chains to baseball bats". As concerning reports suggested the movie was triggering anarchy and violence, Paramount's vice president Gordon Weaver told Herman the studio would, after a six-day pause, resume advertising in a muted fashion, merely providing screening times and locations.

The original marketing memorably depicted numerous gang members with accompanying text that confirms "These are the Armies of the Night. They are 100,000 strong. They outnumber the cops five to one. They could run New York City - Tonight they're all out to get the Warriors".

It grabbed juicy headlines for a short while - a Californian teenager shot in the head at a Palm Springs drive-in, a gang of youths terrorising subway passengers at 42nd Street and Eighth Avenue, a construction worker stabbed to death during an intermission, a 16-year-old killed at a Boston theatre. Minor protests were staged at subway stations. Ultimately, like the highly questionable reports of copycat violence linked to everything from *A Clockwork Orange* to Chucky and *Natural Born Killers*, it was useful publicity based on a few idiots just looking for an excuse to do something stupid or lethal. The Sergeant overseeing the investigation of the Palm Springs murder referred to it as a big coincidence that *The Warriors* was involved and, despite Paramount offering to pay for additional security at theatres, and some taking them up on the offer, exhibitors were more likely to downplay the connection between fights breaking out and the movie they were showing. The N.Y.P.D. were quick to deny an increase in gang activity because of *The Warriors*.

With or without the fleeting controversy, the picture's pop culture afterlife has been rich and varied. John Carpenter's *Escape from New York* followed two years later and makes for a marvellously cynical alternate take on thematically and geographically similar territory. Among many homages and parodies to *The Warriors*, the 2014 *The Simpsons* episode *The Winter of His Content* has The Eagles' version of *In the City* appearing within a plot involving a "Bully Summit" at Krustyland and gang clashes on Springfield's beach and subway. Though a TV series and cinematic remake have been mooted at various times and never emerged, its influence can be found in the work of numerous hip-hop artists, a 2005 video game over which Roger Hill took unsuccessful legal action, Funko Pops, board games and Mezco action figures that sported reasonable and rather fetching likenesses for Remar and Beck. You know you'd love playing with them given half the chance!

THESE ARE THE ARMIES OF THE NIGHT.
They are 100,000 strong. They outnumber the cops five to one.
They could run New York City. Tonight they're all out to get the Warriors.

Paramount Pictures Presents A Lawrence Gordon Production "THE WARRIORS"
Executive Producer Frank Marshall Based Upon the Novel by Sol Yurick
Screenplay by David Shaber and Walter Hill Produced by Lawrence Gordon
R RESTRICTED UNDER 17 REQUIRES ACCOMPANYING PARENT OR ADULT GUARDIAN Directed by Walter Hill Read the Dell Book

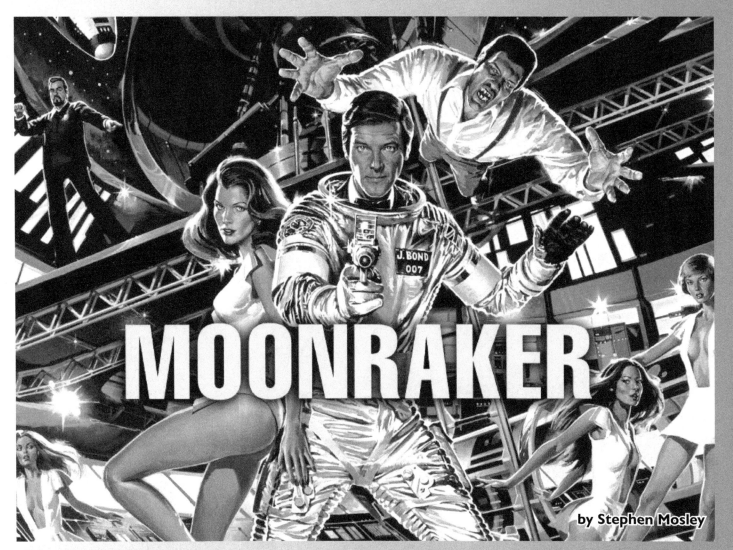

MOONRAKER

by Stephen Mosley

The end credits of *The Spy Who Loved Me* had promised that James Bond would return in *For Your Eyes Only*. However, on noting that the top-grossing films of 1977 (the year of *Spy*'s release) were *Star Wars* and *Close Encounters of the Third Kind*, producer Albert R. Broccoli sought a more intergalactic-sounding title. As luck would have it, the only full-length Ian Fleming Bond novel yet to be filmed was his third, 'Moonraker' (1955). (While the book may have *sounded* like science fiction, its plot was entirely earthbound: Bond has to stop an atomic warhead, concealed upon the titular rocket, from destroying London).

Buoyed by interest from legendary producer Alexander Korda (*Things to Come*, *The Thief of Bagdad*), Fleming had actually written 'Moonraker' with the cinema in mind - even going so far as to adapt the novel into a screenplay himself. Sadly, neither this, nor his original storyline, ever reached the screen. Instead, screenwriter Christopher Wood merely reworked his plot for *The Spy Who Loved Me*. Whereas the former's villain had attempted to create a new underwater race, *Moonraker*'s crazed industrialist, Hugo Drax, would plan a new civilisation in outer space. All that survives from Fleming's source material is a moment wherein Bond and the heroine find themselves trapped beneath a launch vehicle as it prepares for lift-off.

Also returning from *Spy* was director Lewis Gilbert, who kicked off production in February 1978 by capturing footage of the Rio carnival alongside *Spy*'s French cinematographer Claude Renoir. Though, owing to failing eyesight, Renoir would be replaced by his fellow countryman Jean Tournier (*The Day of the Jackal*) when shooting proper began in August.

Over five weeks in May and June of 1978, the second unit, led by John Glen, filmed the breathtaking pre-credits sequence over Yountville, California. Using an idea from executive producer Michael G. Wilson, originally devised for *The Spy Who Loved Me*, Bond is pushed from a plane and pursued through the air by razor-toothed villain Jaws. Back by popular demand, Richard Kiel's character had proven especially popular with *Spy*'s younger viewers. Indeed, it was a suggestion from Lewis Gilbert's grandson that saw Jaws evolve into a good guy by the end of *Moonraker*.

With Jake Lombard and Ron Luginbill standing in for Roger Moore's Bond and Kiel respectively, the result is absolutely spellbinding: the nearest we'll ever get to seeing humans in flight.

Despite one of the best opening moments in the franchise, *Moonraker* is widely regarded as a lesser 007 entry. Steven

Jay Rubin, who gives the film one out of five stars in his 'Complete James Bond Movie Encyclopedia', encapsulates the views of most fans when he writes of "action without credibility" and "just plain stupid... unbelievably dumb moment[s]."

Yet, *Moonraker* would prove to be the biggest box office success of the series until 1995's *GoldenEye* and is a particular favourite of this author.

There's a continental feel to the visuals which sets it aside from other 007 movies. Witness the hazy shafts of sunlight piercing the woodland gloom where Corinne Cléry is devoured by Drax's Dobermans. This memorable scene allegedly prompted Prince Philip to shout at the screen during the Royal Premiere: "Don't go into the woods, you stupid girl!"

The 'continental feel' I refer to is not just a matter of style: For tax reasons, *Moonraker* was a co-production with United Artists' French subsidiary and thus utilised all three of Paris's major studios. Even the familiar office sets of Bond's superior M (Bernard Lee) and his private secretary Miss Moneypenny (Lois Maxwell) were flat-packed and sent to France. The Bond unit's usual stable, Pinewood Studios, would be used only for post-production, most notably Derek Meddings' Oscar-nominated special effects. Part of the deal stipulated that a number of French actors be employed, hence Michael Lonsdale (*The Day of the Jackal*) as Drax, Corinne Cléry (*The Story of O*) as Drax's assistant and Blanche Ravalec as Dolly, the redemptive love interest of Jaws. Contrary to popular belief, Ravalec's character *doesn't* wear braces on her teeth - a classic example of the "Mandela Effect", i.e., the phenomenon of collective false memories.

French locations included Vaux-le-Vicomte, a 17th century chateau on the outskirts of Paris, which doubled as Drax's Californian habitat. It is here that Bond meets CIA agent Dr. Holly Goodhead, played by Lois Chiles.

Despite the silliness of her character's name, Chiles presents a smart and classy foil to 007's outmoded sexism. And, in an unusual turn for Bond girls, she even plays a major part in the climactic action, punching out baddies and piloting the shuttle in which she and Bond make their escape.

"You have to realise this was the '70s and women were very upset about being portrayed as sexual objects," Chiles told 'The New York Times' in 2012. "Wearing that yellow spacesuit during much of the movie didn't make me very alluring," she added. "But it was their concession to the women's movement."

Originally in the running for the role of Anya in *The Spy Who Loved Me*, Chiles was remembered by Lewis Gilbert when he found himself seated next to the Texas-born actress on an American flight. Post-Bond, she would be haunted by 'The Hitchhiker' in *Creepshow 2* (1987), before partaking in one of the best gags of *Austin Powers: International Man of Mystery* (1997) as the bereaved partner of Dr. Evil's steamrolled henchman.

The above title - the most joyous and accomplished of 007 spoofs - owes much to *Moonraker* in its space-age design and somewhat juvenile humour. But while deriding aspects of the latter, *Moonraker*'s critics overlook its more serious moments. Aside from a tense climax, there's a gripping scene where Bond is spun at a deadly pace in a centrifuge machine. The rippling effect this causes upon Moore's face - created by offscreen blasts from an air hose - is quite surprising when one considers how unruffled his superspy usually is. Forsaking any sense of vanity, Moore turns in a convincing show of vulnerability once he escapes the machine. Staggering away, broken and exhausted, he looks visibly disoriented by his death-defying experience. This is acting which flies in the face of critical consensus, typified by John Stanley's review in his 'Creature Features Movie Guide': "Roger Moore walks indifferently through it all." Hardly. (Although, in this author's opinion, Moore gives his very best 007

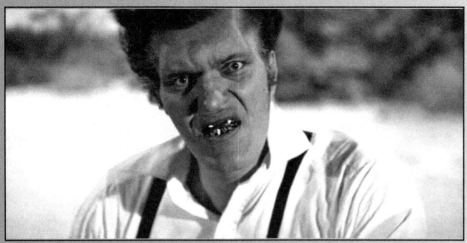

performance in *For Your Eyes Only*).

In September '78, the crew decamped to Venice, where more amusing spectacles unfolded, such as the gondola chase, a double-taking pigeon and, in a blink-and-you'll-miss-it cameo which could have been performed by anyone, comic actor Alfie Bass (*Help!*, *The Fearless Vampire Killers*) as a "consumptive Italian". There's even a nod to *Close Encounters of the Third Kind* when that film's famed five-note leitmotif is used as a passcode to a secret laboratory. As legend has it, Broccoli requested use of the music from Steven Spielberg himself. When Spielberg later sought permission to use the James Bond Theme in *The Goonies* (1985), Broccoli reportedly told him, "There are more than five notes in the 007 theme."

The humour inherent in *Moonraker*'s Venetian sequences is not wholly surprising when one learns that additional dialogue was provided, uncredited, by comedy writers Dick Clement and Ian La Frenais; the creators of *Porridge* and *The Likely Lads* would make a more substantial, yet equally anonymous, contribution to the 'unofficial' Bond film *Never Say Never Again* (1983).

Less hilarious was Moore's collapse after Christmas with kidney stones. A martyr to this painful condition since his first Bond outing *Live and Let Die* (1973), production was held up for four days in order for the actor to recover. As Broccoli quipped to the 'Daily Express': "To think the future of my $30 million movie is hanging on a goddam pebble."

Once Moore had passed the pebble, he arrived at the next location Rio de Janeiro in January 1979 (in fact, footage of Moore's arrival is used in the film). Despite his recent infirmity, the 51-year-old actor threw himself into the action sequences with his usual vigour, including a thrilling tussle with Jaws atop a cable car - a stunt in which Moore's double Richard Graydon, working without a harness, almost lost his life.

The cable car fight climaxes with Jaws crashing through a shopfront advertising

7-Up. Indeed, throughout the Rio scenes, there is product placement galore. One villainous lackey even has his head smashed into the mouth of a stewardess on a British Airways billboard ("We'll take more care of you"). While this has created further disdain for the movie, one has to remember that Ian Fleming himself peppered the Bond novels with brand names as a means of grounding his fantasies in recognisable settings. The author is very careful to note, for example, that 007 lights his Morland cigarettes with a Ronson lighter, whilst wearing a dark-blue Sea Island shirt and driving a vintage Bentley. So, perhaps he would have approved of Jaws inadvertently promoting soda?

Principal photography wrapped in February 1979 and John Barry added his superlative music score. Although the title song, sung by Shirley Bassey (her third after *Goldfinger* and *Diamonds Are Forever*), is somewhat lacklustre, the remainder of Barry's themes more than make up for this, especially the majestic *Flight into Space*.

Released in June 1979, *Moonraker* would sadly be the final entry for two series' mainstays: Production designer Ken Adam (who'd go on to win an Oscar for *The Madness of King George*, 1994) and actor Bernard Lee. Having turned to alcohol following a string of personal tragedies - including the death of his wife in a housefire and a violent mugging - Lee died of stomach cancer in January 1981.

As with *The Spy Who Loved Me*, a Christopher Wood-penned novelization, 'James Bond and Moonraker', was issued by Panther Books. Wood's prose remolds the smooth cinematic Bond of Moore into the scar-faced "blunt instrument" of Fleming. Indeed, the whole novel reads like a Fleming original, with lines like: "Bond... smoked his fiftieth cigarette of the day." (Fleming's Bond seems to subsist on a diet of fags, booze and scrambled eggs. It's a wonder he was ever fit enough for any assignment).

Taking a leaf from Wood's book, Broccoli also decided to reintroduce elements of Fleming into the more grounded adventure promised by *Moonraker*'s closing credits: This time, it really would be *For Your Eyes Only*.

Outer space now belongs to 007.

Albert R. Broccoli
presents
ROGER MOORE
is
JAMES BOND 007
in Ian Fleming's
MOONRAKER

Co-Starring Lois Chiles Richard Kiel as 'Jaws' Michael Lonsdale as 'Drax'
Produced by Albert R. Broccoli Directed by Lewis Gilbert Screenplay by Christopher Wood
Music by John Barry Production Design by Ken Adam

United Artists
A Transamerica Company

TAKING OFF

by Allen Rubinstein

Ah, sweet freedom. Reject the squares, smoke some dope, grow your hair long and leave Sunday mass in the rearview mirror. Hit the open road. Join a commune. Cue The Beatles:

> Silently closing her bedroom door.
> Leaving the note that she hoped would say more.
> She goes down the stairs to the kitchen
> Clutching her handkerchief.
> Quietly turning the backdoor key.
> Stepping outside, she is free.
> She ... "We gave her most of our lives."
> Is leaving ... "Sacrificed most of our lives."
> Home ... "We gave her everything money could buy."

Paul McCartney wrote *She's Leaving Home* after reading the story of Melanie Coe, a teenager from South London who, after growing up steeped in luxury, remarked: "My father and mother never once told me they loved me." Coe was one of hundreds of thousands pulling away from the conservative values and institutions of their elders, a phenomenon of "runaway teens" as the media termed it.

Concern for their welfare and general social alarm grew to the point of legislation - Congress' Runaway Youth Act of 1974, which set up funding and a small agency (which still exists) to help these kids before they got into too much trouble. Looking back at this moment of middle-class panic can be almost charming, understanding that the word 'homeless' meant something far different than it does now, and most of those errant youth are on the cusp of collecting Social Security. They had their journey in that personal space between the heat of the moment and the larger historical context, and then they went home, wherever home turned out to be.

A film made during the period about this issue could easily be a treacly movie of the week, dripping with manufactured drama. Instead, Miloš Forman's *Taking Off* is a delicate, honest, wry blooming flower of a story that ought to top anyone's list of unjustly forgotten '70s gems. *Taking Off* does so much with so little - an unexpected take on "freedom", not as some trite generation gap conflict or hippie fantasy, but as a look at genuine human beings in the midst of their own unique and expanding life experience.

As it happens, at the time of making *Taking Off*, Forman

was having his own involuntary life experience of freedom. After coming of age as a war orphan (his mother, father and stepfather died in Nazi death camps), Forman received some of the best education Czechoslovakia offered. The high school meant for war orphans was so well funded that government elites would scramble to get their own children admitted. Pursuing theater, he enrolled at FAMU (Film Faculty of the Academy of Arts) where he began creating films with most of the eventual directors of the fabled '60s Czech New Wave. Bridging that creative peak of Soviet-Bloc filmmaking directly into the thriving New Hollywood scene is as much Forman's legacy as his two Best Picture Oscars.

The Wave, as such bursts of creativity often do, emerged alongside political upheaval. Both film and literature of the time contributed to rising criticism and public protest over four decades of single-party Communist rule. These directors specifically rejected the stuffy official style of 'Socialist Realism' which forbade criticism of the state and demanded the submersion of any overt film technique, such as montage, that would call attention to a specific authorial hand behind a film. With an output some fifty films deep over a mere six years, many New Wave contributions, such as Forman's merciless institutional sendup *The Firemen's Ball* (1967), were thinly-disguised or metaphorical rebukes of the Party. While struggles with the Censorship Board were rife (*Firemen's Ball* was banned for several years once President Antonin Novotny screened and loathed it), Party leadership had more pressing uprisings to deal with, allowing the Wave to continue.

Taking Off owes more to Forman's two earlier movies -

Black Peter (1964) and *Loves of a Blonde* (1965). Both are coming-of-age stories with a remarkable ear for natural dialogue and moments of social awkwardness. They are light-hearted and authentic, poking at human foibles. They don't emphasize institutional critique, but they have fun at the expense of authority figures and general propriety, while their young protagonists are at a loss to navigate life at the direction of generally clueless adults. In other words, Forman was on the forefront of the counterculture.

Unlike *Taking Off* though, Forman's three Czech features were enormously successful, landing two Academy nominations for Best Foreign Language Film and establishing him as a major international filmmaker. The next move for the ambitious director was to enter the much larger, more profitable American market. He had visited New York City and was captivated by the turbulent protest activity seemingly everywhere, the vibrant culture taking over the East Village and especially the musical *Hair*, which would take him another decade to adapt to film. Forman set out to create an American debut that centered on the changing mores of youth culture and recruited heralded French screenwriter Jean-Claude Carriére to co-create.

Forman and Carriére stayed in Paris, developing the script for what would become *Taking Off* when the foundations of Forman's life suddenly crumbled. The Czech public unrest of the '60s had become the Prague Spring reforms of February 1968, which then inspired the Warsaw Pact invasion of August 1968. 500,000 troops primarily from the Soviet Union poured into the country. The government, caught flat-footed, was quickly deposed, and the authoritarian Communist wing put in charge. Forman's homeland was in chaos, tanks occupying the

streets, with reformists and subversives rounded up for indefinite incarceration. The Czech New Wave came to an abrupt end.

Without a full picture of what was happening, Forman flew back and joined his lifelong friend and collaborator Ivan Passer. Both were married and separated. Forman was the father of twin boys he was forced to leave behind with their mother, not seeing them for many years. He and Passer quickly decided to flee, and they drove to the Austrian border without the exit visas they now needed to leave the country. When they got there, with no plan how to get through, the well-known Forman was recognized by a soldier who loved his movies, excitedly describing key scenes to his fellow guards. With 300,000 Czechs in various stages of emigrating, a movie fan at the right place and time waved Forman and Passer through without official papers. They left behind the majority of their New Wave compatriots who were prohibited from making films for decades.

Back in New York, on a work visa from Paramount Pictures, a marooned Czech director, his Czech cinematographer (Forman's regular cameraman Miroslav Ondříček) with a screenplay from a French writer, and an African-American editor (more on him later) created a movie about an average white suburban couple with a missing daughter. It's astonishing, given all this background, how straightforwardly American *Taking Off* turned out. Rewrites from John Klein and John Guare likely helped, but watching it, no US citizen would mistake this for, say, the Euro-coated pantomime of Antonioni's *Zabriskie Point* (1970) and *The Passenger* (1975).

Even so, Forman later referred to *Taking Off* as "my last Czech film", which rings true for its filmmaking techniques more than its portrayal of Americans. His Czech pictures share the methods more associated with independent regional filmmaking - extended set pieces with loose structure, non-professional actors for smaller parts, improvisation and studying communities in large crowd scenes. In later work, Forman aspired to making more traditional American films of greater scope and portent, succeeding spectacularly with *One Flew Over the Cuckoo's Nest, Amadeus, Ragtime* and others. However, I would argue that it's the merging of American and Czech sensibilities that makes *Taking Off* so special.

The film's initial creative choices work brilliantly in its favor. *Taking Off* tells us about the Tyne family and their fifteen-year-old daughter Jeannie, played by Linnea Heacock. The daughter barely has a dozen lines of dialogue. The story is not hers, but her parents Lynn (Lynn Carlin) and Larry (Buck Henry, in a rare leading role). Jeannie lies to them to attend an open-call music audition in the city, comes back that evening altered on something, then slips out the door again. What happens with Lynn and Larry in the meantime is the film's main focus.

In the opening scenes, Forman and Carriére do something quite remarkable, intercutting Jeannie's music audition with Lynn and Larry's dawning dread that their 'baby' is unaccounted for. The audition sequence is based on an even earlier project of Forman's, the 1963 quasi-documentary *Konkurs (The Audition)* where he and Passer held tryouts for a fake female singer and recorded the ambitious young girls who responded. Forman can only have moved the stunt to New York here, since the faces, performances and various stumbling attempts to sing are so obviously the real deal. Those 1971 hairstyles and clothing, the mix of period specific, often self-written music, the varying levels of maturity, confidence and professionalism, the dynamics of a large room of very nervous strangers - why stage any of it when holding auditions is already a director's natural territory?

This collection of song performances crackles with energy, and here the work of editor John Carter must be called out. This was only Carter's third feature, his previous being the major MLK documentary *KING - A Filmed Record... Montgomery to Memphis*, but before he embarked on a lengthy career cutting movies, he was the first black editor ever to work in New York television as part of *The Ed Sullivan Show*. In one three-minute sequence, Carter mixes fifty separate renditions of The Montanas' single *Let's Get a Little Sentimental* into a single performance, some girls onscreen for as little as one or two words of the lyric. Some forget the words or drift off, and poor Jeannie chokes. Seeing the faces staring back at her, she can't even get started. The editing throughout *Taking Off* is a high point, even outside those kind of showy montages, returning to more clips of young ladies singing throughout.

The audition does two more things relevant to the story being told. First, it sets the larger stage of the film, the countercultural preoccupations. The credits run under the lyrics "I believe, and believe, and believe, and believe, and believe, and believe, and believe in love, love, love, love, love, love." Carly Simon shows up to sing about getting stoned because the "short term physical effects are so groovy", and none other than a very young Kathy Bates trills out a complex fairy tale song called "Even the Horses Had Wings" as a note of childhood innocence drifting away like vapor.

The second important thing is that, while we watch Lynn and Larry panicking about where Jeannie might be, we simultaneously see where she actually is. She isn't *missing*; she knows exactly where she is. Jeannie is *fine*. Her parents don't have to fear for her safety even though we know they will anyway. It redefines Lynn's tears of worry from a mystery yearning for answers to her first step on the road to letting go.

The reality of runaway children was them wresting freedom from their family, and for sure in many cases, their

liberation from a toxic household was fully warranted. At the same time, who in all the news stories considered the parent's freedom from their kids? It almost sounds like a joke, but *Taking Off* addresses the idea seriously and honestly.

During their search for Jeannie, Larry and Lynn come across the S.P.F.C. - the (fictional) Society for the Parents of Fugitive Children - through Ann Lockston (Audra Lindley), a woman whose child ran off seven months ago. She has this to say: "I don't feel responsible. Everything that happens to us in life is… Well, it's just another life experience, and we should get everything out of it we can… Ben, that's my husband, we found that just since Nancy's been gone, and looking for her, it's brought us closer together. Our relationship is closer, more profound."

So, Lynn and Larry decide to go out and have fun for a change, spending the night at a hotel where Ike and Tina Turner are furiously performing. Soon they join a large conference of the S.P.F.C. where the themes of the film start to come together. "Friends, as you know, the purpose and the aim of our society is not only to try to find those children, but to try to understand them … and perhaps the greatest difficulty that we face lies in the urges and pressures that lead our children into the taking of drugs."

They introduce Dr. Besh as a speaker, who's an apparent expert on such things, then immediately cut to a later, smaller gathering elsewhere in the hotel. He tells them that the earlier talk the film cuts away from is truthful, but useless. "For you to understand what your youngster is going through, you really need to have to have a similar experience." In the centerpiece of the movie, the leadership of the S.P.F.C. pull out a plastic bag of joints and pass them around, proposing an experiment. Conducting it is a patient of the doctor who is an experienced pot smoker, played by long-faced actor Vincent Schiavelli. In a single scene, under a puff of curly hair, dressed in a very '70s puce and lavender suit, Schiavelli steals the film.

He clinically teaches everyone how to inhale a joint and how bogarting is considered very rude. Smoke filling the air, Schiavelli starts yet another music cue, playing the atmospheric song *Air* by The Incredible String Band and proceeds to coach a room full of middle-aged squares through their first high. "That's all you have to do; just breathe. Let the rhythm of the music take you. Do whatever you feel like. Relax and let it happen. Don't sit on it. Let it fly. Just dig your whole body floating away." Every second of it, every reaction is priceless and hilarious. As one online critic put it: "Nobody observes faces like Miloš Forman."

The man who pulls out the bag of grass mentions that he's a lawyer, and what he's proposing to do that evening (an "indulgence" as he puts it) is illegal. Then they do it anyway. Not a single person in the crowded room judges the exercise or resists participating in it, and this is pointedly after the grave hush that falls over the larger conference when they mention the urges and pressures that lead their children into the taking of drugs. They all drink alcohol, which is a drug. They enjoy being high, and it's clear from their responses that they have been curious. Suddenly, they have permission. The S.P.F.C. gives them a framework and a rationalization to make trying the mind-altering substance okay - to follow the same path of experiential freedom their absent kids are on. The context these parents (and the audience in the theater watching *Taking Off*) no doubt had was the nightly news, portraying the scourge of escalating pot smoking. The only thing separating them from the younger generation is their faith in those messages that are supposed to keep them in a box of respectability and legality. With one ready excuse, those mental blocks dissolve.

The film curiously chooses not to focus on the Tynes during the pot smoking scene, but the fallout from it is all theirs. They arrive home with their new friends, Ann and Ben Lockston, laughing and drinking without a care in the world, upon which Ben (Paul Benedict) starts a game of low-card strip. Indications are that the Tynes are about to get a life experience they won't soon forget with some '70s swingers. I won't describe the state they're in when Jeannie, having simply come home on her own, walks in on them, but it's why audiences went to movies in the '70s instead of watching TV.

It turns out that Jeannie didn't land the audition, but she did land the rock star Jamie. The musician/singer/songwriter, only seen in brief shots during the audition sequence, is who Jeannie spent the past few weeks with. Putting his clothes back on, Larry insists he come to meet them over dinner and, on arriving, Jamie is a pile of hair in a hippie blouse and considerably older than Jeannie. In a sweet moment, Lynn has a wonderfully acted private meltdown seeing her little girl with someone so outside her world, and Larry tenderly pulls her out of it.

The ensuing dinner is cringingly awkward, and Jamie says very little. That's until Larry openly asks him how much money he makes as a musician. "Last year I made $290,000." Larry nearly spits out his glass of wine. That's higher than two million in today's money. Jamie gruffly lays out his entire rationale, "Yeah, you see a lot of things that the government is doing that make you kinda angry, and you write some songs about it, and you try to reach as many people as you can, and in the end, you end up paying for those very same things that made you angry in the first place. But I guess I accept contradictions." He finishes by mentioning that he's saving up to buy an intercontinental ballistic missile to try to balance nuclear power among nations.

This casually political disclosure winds up the story. The new boyfriend has the one quality that can lay to rest any and all concerns of an average American white suburban couple - he may be hairy but he's also rich. Apparently, Jeannie instinctively knows how to pick 'em. They ask him to sing something, but Jamie doesn't think he can "get his rocks off" so Larry sings instead - a rousing rendition of *Stranger in Paradise*. This music-saturated story, after all, is all about Lynn and Larry learning a bit about who they are without their daughter and learning to sing out loud.

When you combine the backstory of *Taking Off* with its content, it's genuinely impressive how much it captures in the grand sweep of history - the yearning for freedom from tyranny, freedom to determine one's own fate and leadership,

freedom to express and create, to explore and experiment, to break taboos and discover oneself, and the freedom to just *take off* for something that's calling you without interfering family members hunting you down like some lost possession. The sheer economy of its five or six set pieces to tell a simple family story is in its time and of its time and quite perceptive about human behavior. From its opening frame, you are in the hands of a supremely confident director who just "gets it" and has no interest in the cliches of the day. It's really a shame that the film didn't gain an audience. If *Taking Off* is any indication, American movies could use a lot more Czech New Wave.

Aerial Mayhem: Italian Style –
CONCORDE AFFAIR

by Bryan C. Kuriawa

If one thing can be said about Italian movie producers, it's that the cash-in was a staple of many of their productions in the post-war era. Whether it was sword and sandal epics, poliziotteschi outings, spaghetti westerns or various horror genres, if there was a popular trend and cash to be made, the Italians would clamber over themselves to strike a deal.

Surprisingly, the disaster genre rarely appeared on any Italian producer's radar. It may have been a heyday for disaster pics in America (thanks to epics like *The Poseidon Adventure* and *The Towering Inferno*) and Japanese audiences may have flocked to 'Panic Films' like *Prophecies of Nostradamus*, *The Bullet Train* and *Mainline to Terror*, but Italian studios steered clear of creating cinematic apocalypses of their own despite their clear popularity. Among the few that domestic and overseas audiences got to experience were *The Day the Sky Exploded* (1958) and the Carlo Ponti-produced outing *The Cassandra Crossing* (1976).

Yet in 1979, producers Mino Loy and Luciano Martino decided to cash in on an upcoming American disaster epic with one of their own. Featuring a unique international cast and helmed by one of the most controversial filmmakers of all time, the results were anything but uninteresting.

"*We Have Lost Contact With The Concorde 820*"

Off the French protectorate of Martinique, Concorde Flight 820 is on route to Caracas, Venezuela, with only its two pilots, a flight engineer and two flight attendants on board. All of a sudden, Flight 820 loses contact with local air control and falls into a dive before crashing into the sea.

Meanwhile in New York City, a high-ranking executive of a multinational airline named Milland (Joseph Cotten) and his associate Danker (Edmund Purdom) wait over news of 820's disappearance.

Shortly after, freelance writer Moses Brody (James Franciscus) receives word from his ex-wife Nicole (Mag Fleming) that something big is happening on Martinique. She suggests he should come down and check it out for himself. When he arrives, he learns she has died of a heart attack. As a result, his only lead is her friend George (Francisco Charles) who tells him that just before her death Nicole had learned of something unusual being conducted offshore. George also informs him that two of his fishermen friends went missing off the coast around the same time.

As Moses investigates, Milland learns that a flight attendant from 820, Jean Beneyton (Mimsy Farmer), survived the crash. She is now being held for ransom by his associate Forsythe (Venantino Venantini) on his yacht off Martinique. In the meantime, a Latin American airline plans to fly their first Concorde with 100 passengers from Rio De Janeiro to London in the coming days. In reality, Moses isn't just looking for a story, he's in a race against time.

own Concorde-themed aerial thriller. With a similarly all-star cast, location shooting in the US and Martinique and the support of British Aerospace, the question was how Deodato would fare at creating a disaster epic.

"The Idea We've Got To Get Across Is That The Concorde Is Actually An Unsafe Machine"

From the '60s through the late '80s, many American and European actors would migrate to Italy for movie and TV roles. As a result, Deodato found himself working with a unique cast of classic Hollywood faces and the new guard.

Most well-remembered for his role in *Beneath the Planet of the Apes*, Franciscus delivers a strong performance as Moses Brody. A down-on-his-luck reporter, thrust into the Concorde saga by his ex-wife's mysterious death, he's dedicated to learning the truth at all costs.

A familiar fixture on American TV with shows including *Mr. Novak*, *Longstreet*, *Doc Elliot* and *Hunter*, he was always in demand. In 1971, he went over to Italy for the first time for Dario Argento's second feature *Cat O' Nine Tails*. He would return on several occasions, including for 1979's *Killer Fish* and the *Jaws* clone *Great White* (1981). *Concorde Affair* wasn't his only disaster outing, as he also appeared in the Canadian film *City on Fire* that same year and Irwin Allen's final theatrical epic *When Time Ran Out* in 1980.

While Franciscus thrived in post-war Hollywood,

An engaging thriller, *Concorde Affair* is one of the lesser-known disaster outings from that decade of mayhem. Directed by Ruggero Deodato, it proved a unique film for a director who would soon after shock the cinematic world permanently.

"Long Live The Free Press"

If you look up "controversial" in many movie guides, the name Ruggero Deodato will be front and center. Before achieving notoriety making audiences think twice about jungle trips with *Cannibal Holocaust* and house parties with *The House on the Edge of the Park*, his career was a lot different.

He worked as an assistant director during the '60s, and made his directorial debut with the superhero film *Phenomenal and the Treasure of Tutankhamen* (1968). Following his next feature, the jungle girl adventure *Gungala, La Pantera Nuda* (1968), his career would be rather eclectic for the next decade.

Whether it was historical productions like 1969's *Zenabel*, the erotic thriller *Waves of Lust* (1975) or the buddy cop outing *Live Like a Cop, Die Like a Man* (1976), his output was notable for its variety. In the late '70s, with the fourth Airport film on the way (*The Concorde… Airport '79*), producer Giorgio Carlo Rossi decided to make his

Mimsy Farmer was a creative exile living in Europe. After appearing as a '60s wild chick in such films as *Hot Rods to Hell* (1966) and *Riot on Sunset Strip* (1967), she became disillusioned with the roles she was being offered and moved permanently to Europe where she began taking on more challenging characters such as 1970's *The Road to Salina*. While she appeared in numerous European productions, she gained fame with cult horror fans in Italian giallos such as *Four Flies on Grey Velvet* (1971), *The Perfume of the Lady in Black* (1974) and *Autopsy* (1975). A uniquely attractive and compelling character-actress, Farmer's Jean is the key to the events as they occur, much like the random occurrences or coincidences of a giallo. She's a tortured individual, trying to make sense of her ordeal, as various factions want to use her to their desired ends. Farmer also benefits from good on-screen chemistry with Franciscus's Brody. Reportedly, Franciscus attempted to seduce Mimsy early on, but Deodato said she quickly put him in his place.

In terms of villains, we have two unique Hollywood actors in the form of Cotten and Purdom. Most well remembered for his work with Orson Welles on *Citizen Kane* and *The Magnificent Ambersons*, Cotten was a familiar presence in multiple films during the '40s and '50s.

Towards the end of the '60s, Cotten began travelling overseas for roles, including the Spanish western *White Comanche* (1968) starring William Shatner and Toho's English-language sci-fi production *Latitude Zero* (1969). During the subsequent decade, Cotten appeared in several Italian films including *Lady Frankenstein* (1971), *Baron Blood* (1972) and *Island of The Fishmen* (1979) among others. As Milland, Cotten is a shadowy menace. Viewing the Concorde as a threat to his entire corporation, he refers to what they're involved in as a war and makes comparisons to being an international state. Interestingly, Cotten had also appeared in 1977's *Airport '77*, making him one of the few stars to appear in both the official series and the cash-in.

As his associate Danker, Purdom has that distinctly British way about him, while portraying a reluctant participant in Milland's plot. An import to the Hollywood studio system, he had been marked for superstardom after the success of 1954's *The Student Prince*. However, a string of box-office failures including *The Egyptian* (1954) and *The Prodigal* (1955) soured his future prospects. Coupled with his tabloid-headline personal life, he would leave Hollywood and eventually move to Italy. Appearing in multiple Italian and European films, including the Spanish cult classic *Pieces* (1982), Purdom even attempted his own quasi-directorial effort in the British slasher outing *Don't Open Till Christmas* (1984).

Bringing up the supporting rear are the two furthest opposites in terms of acting careers, Van Johnson and Robert Kerman. The epitome of Hollywood's studio system, Johnson also migrated to Italy for roles in various productions including *Eagles Over London* (1969), *From Corleone to Brooklyn* (1979) and *Killer Crocodile* (1989). He does a fine job as the pilot of the second Concorde which Milland intends to destroy during its inaugural flight.

Known as Dr. Harold Monroe in Deodato's *Cannibal Holocaust* and for his work as an adult film star on such

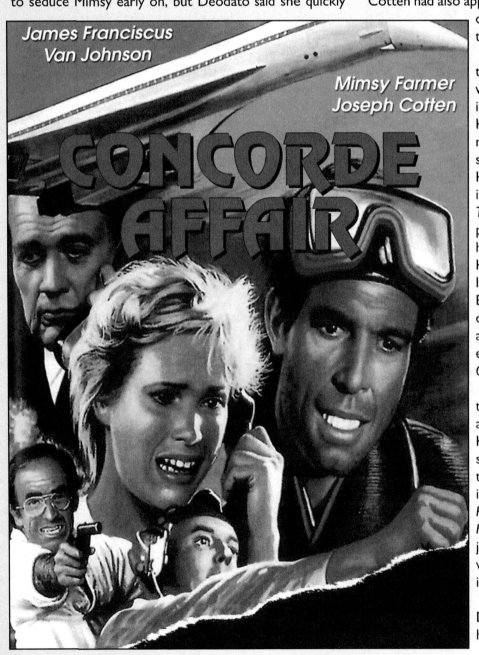

James Franciscus
Van Johnson
Mimsy Farmer
Joseph Cotten
CONCORDE AFFAIR

SOS Concorde

JAMES FRANCISCUS MIMSY FARMER VAN JOHNSON JOSEPH COTTEN
Mise en scène par R. DEODATO pour DANIA FILM-NATIONAL CINEMATOGRAFICA
une sélection C.A.A. distribuée par U.G.C./F.D.C.

JAMES FRANCISCUS | MIMSY FARMER | VAN JOHNSON | JOSEPH COTTEN

productions as *Debbie Does Dallas* (1978) and *Liquid A$$ets* (1982), Robert Kerman's career was a unique one. A trained actor, Kerman worked in the adult film industry - under the pseudonyms Richard Bolla and R. Bolla - during its theatrical Golden Age of the late '70s and early '80s. He would also appear under his real name in Hollywood productions including *The Goodbye Girl* (1977) and *Night of the Creeps* (1986) among other TV and film roles.

According to Kerman, he appeared in a small role in the New-York set Italian production *Blue Nude* (1978). The same individual who cast him in *Nude* asked if he and any of his friends wanted to appear in another production. Bringing along two adult film co-stars, he shot his scenes as a London flight controller with the dialogue written right in front of him. These scenes were possibly shot at Newark Liberty International Airport in New Jersey (as the film thanks the airport's flight control for its cooperation in the end credits).

Impressed with him, Deodato went on to cast Kerman in *Cannibal Holocaust*, which led to starring roles in two subsequent Italian cannibal films by Umberto Lenzi, *Eaten Alive* (1980) and *Cannibal Ferox* (1981). Unfortunately, he was unable to leave New York City for *Ferox* due to labor restrictions and all his scenes were shot there. Any further Italian roles soured when his career as an adult film star was discovered by producers in Rome. While his performance is dubbed over by a British voice actor, Kerman brings a lot of gravitas to his brief role and it's understandable why Deodato thought highly of him. Incidentally, he also appeared as an air traffic controller in *Airport '79* soon after his role in *Concorde Affair*. He could certainly boast an unusual set of connections between the world of adult movies and cinematic aerial disasters.

"We Too Are A Nation... A Multinational State"

Behind the camera, Deodato does an excellent job and crafts a very effective atmosphere for the onscreen events. His direction is very fluid, working well within the various set pieces, characters and locales.

Milland and his cronies are kept to their New York City high rise office, often filmed at a distance while they're making their plans. These closed-off spaces resemble a world of intricacy and secret maneuvering. At the same time, the underwater sequences exploring the downed Concorde are atmospheric, benefiting from the strong photography of Lorenzo Battaglia and Stelvio Cipriani's excellent score. This same intensity can be felt during the opening Concorde's crash, both in terms of framing and editing.

At the same time, the screenplay by Ernesto Gastaldi and Renzo Genta presents some interesting ideas under its disaster thriller narrative. While the plot and characters are enjoyable, the plans of Milland and his associates raise some unique real-world questions.

In the '70s, the race to develop supersonic passenger aircraft (SST) was a major aviation topic as multiple nations involved themselves. America's Boeing was forced to drop out due to an inability to secure state support, while Russia's Tu-144 struggled during its several years of operation. Meanwhile, many American airlines looked to the development of the Anglo-French Concorde with trepidation.

As it made its debut in 1976, numerous environmental groups began protesting the Concorde. Claiming it ran the risk of causing damage to local air quality and the ozone layer due to the sound generated on takeoff, they managed to get it restricted to specific airports, limiting its profitability and routes.

It's unclear where these groups got their funding for such elaborate protests during this era. We know in recent years that oil companies sponsored many of the anti-nuclear power groups during that same decade. Perhaps the Italian screenwriters weren't too far off in their fantasy of unscrupulous businessmen worried about a little competition.

"*Directed By Ruggero Deodato*"

Released in Italy in March 1979, the film proved profitable with Deodato citing it as being more successful internationally than the Airport sequel it was competing against.

While *Concorde Affair* did appear on British and Dutch VHS releases, an American release seemed unlikely. For several years, a bootleg DVD from a company called Televista, using a poor VHS source with severe ghosting, was the only available option and is still available on some websites. Then in 2013, Italian cult film buffs made a curious discovery.

The German home video company Ascot Elite Home Entertainment released a Region B Blu-Ray of the film under its theatrical title *Das Concorde Inferno*. Not only did Ascot get a remastered print from a 35mm source, but the original English-language audio track featuring the performances of Franciscus,

Farmer, Cotten, Johnson and Purdom was included. Now Deodato's Techniscope-lensed scenes and Battaglia's underwater photography can be seen in their full glory. It would be nice if a new English-language disc could be released by a company like Severin Films or Kino Lorber Studio Classics, as most don't have the option to run region-locked Blu-rays.

In the end, Deodato's *Concorde Affair* is an effective disaster thriller and well-deserving of a proper retrospective. Buttressed by the legacy of *Cannibal Holocaust*, and ignored even in Harvey Fenton's biography of Deodato, it's a movie that adds an additional layer to his multilayered career. Attempting to compete with Hollywood's disaster outings, Deodato crafts a unique film that further showcases his ability as a director.

Before delving into a world of cannibals and horror that would mark his subsequent career, Deodato proved himself more than capable of matching his Hollywood counterparts. Even at supersonic speeds!

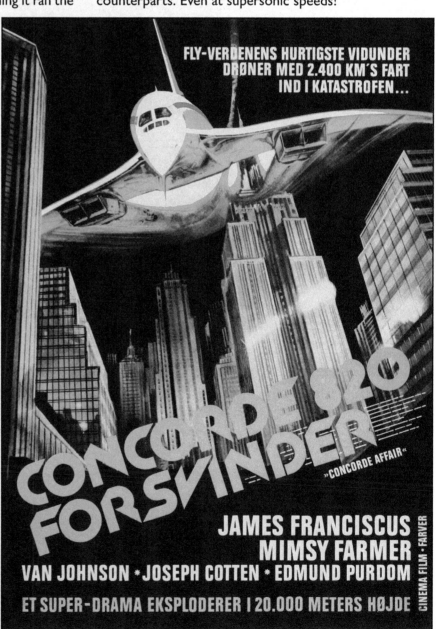

FLY-VERDENENS HURTIGSTE VIDUNDER DRØNER MED 2.400 KM´S FART IND I KATASTROFEN...

CONCORDE 80 FORSVINDER

"CONCORDE AFFAIR"

JAMES FRANCISCUS
MIMSY FARMER
VAN JOHNSON * JOSEPH COTTEN * EDMUND PURDOM
ET SUPER-DRAMA EKSPLODERER I 20.000 METERS HØJDE

CINEMA FILM · FARVER

THE BLACK PRINCE OF SHADOWS

A LOOK AT THE BLACULA MOVIES

by Simon J. Ballard

It could have gone so differently. With a punning title like *Blacula,* you would expect something with its tongue firmly in cheek as it rides the Blaxploitation craze, and that is very nearly what was going to happen until William Marshall - as the titular vampire - stepped in and decided the whole situation required a touch of class. Rather like Robert Quarry did with the Count Yorga films, which is a highly pertinent comparison to make since the shot of Yorga's coffin in a crate being lifted onto the back of a pick-up truck is reused here as, er, Blacula's coffin in a crate being lifted into the back of a pick-up truck.

Comedy-action movie *Cotton Comes to Harlem* kick-started the Blaxploitation genre in 1970, the term itself a pejorative label created in 1972 by Junius Griffin, who was at the time the president of the Beverly Hills-Hollywood National Association for the Advancement of Colored [sic] People, or the NAACP. As far as he was concerned, movies such as *Super Fly* and *Shaft* were responsible for "proliferating offenses" to the black community due to negative stereotypes and their involvement with crime.

Away from such controversies, it was certainly true that such features attracted widespread popularity all over the world and in no time American International Pictures took note and decided they wanted a piece of the action. With their long history in horror, such as Roger Corman's Edgar Allan Poe cycle, this seemed to be the obvious route to take, and *Blacula* would become the first of around eight horror films in the '70s within the Blaxploitation field upon its release in August 1972.

William Crain was hired to direct, his first film after handling intern duties on *Brother John*, a rather curious drama about an African American who turns up whenever a relative is about to pass away. He would see the rest of his career mainly in television.

Scripting duties were assigned to Raymond Koenig (this and the sequel being his only screen credits) and Joan Torres, author of the non-fiction book 'Men Who Hate Women and the Women Who Love Them'. She noted: "Whenever a horror film was playing, the place was packed with African American families who would scream and laugh and have a rollicking good time." She and Koenig were Jewish, and therefore perhaps related to the discrimination the black populace of America suffered from. They tasked their friend Wallace Sides, a black illustrator from South Central Los Angeles (L.A. was where *Blacula* would be filmed), to help with the dialogue.

Torres would balk at the term Blaxploitation, preferring to see the picture merely as a vampire film that had a black cast, but to be honest when two white writers create a story involving a largely black cast for minor studio AIP, the term does rather fit! Their main character was initially named Andrew Brown, but theatre turned TV actor Marshall had other ideas, and worked closely with the makers of the movie to give greater dignity to the part he was asked to play.

A whole backstory was created for the character renamed Mamuwalde, of the Abani tribe northwest of the Niger Delta. An effective prologue was created in which Mamuwalde and his bride Luva visit Count Dracula at his castle in Transylvania in 1780, with a rather impoverished set that only goes to highlight just how marvellous the set designers were at Hammer. Charles Macaulay is rather good in the part, however, and his white hair and beard hit the mark as far as comparisons to the 1897 novel are concerned.

Obviously, there is no way Dracula is going to concede to his guest's demands that he ends the black slave trade, and in retaliation for Mamuwalde's disparaging remarks upon his manners the Prince of Darkness turns the African prince into a vampire before sealing him in a coffin where he will rage with a hunger for blood for all eternity, his wife locked in beside him where she may cry until death becomes her. That is a bit bad mannered, to be fair.

As *Dracula A.D. 1972* would segue from Victorian London to the '70s via the sudden appearance of an aeroplane in the sky, so *Blacula* would transform from the eighteenth century to the present day through s funky jazz opening theme playing out to some basic animation as a red blob of blood transforms into a naked woman harangued by a swooping bat. The soundtrack was provided by Gene Page, who worked in the fields of R&B, soul, funk and jazz among others, and The Hues Corporation - a Black American pop and soul trio consisting of Karl Russell, H. Ann Kelley and St. Clair Lee - appeared as themselves in nightclub scenes.

Away from any potential racial stereotypes, our first encounter in current times is with antique hunters Bobby and Billy, a black and white gay couple who are frankly so outrageously camp and flamboyant, they don't walk - they flounce!

Mind you, I'm a gay man and I've done my fair share of mincing so personally I'm not that offended. Quite the opposite - to have two gay men so in love with each other and whose sexuality is there just because, and not made a feature of, was nicely radical for 1972. At that point, the first Gay Pride had only just occurred two years before, so as with Jewish writers Torres and Koenig and the largely black cast, it's a case of repressed sufferers uniting!

Bobby and Billy have bought Dracula's possessions. "Where we come from, Dracula is the crème de la crème of camp!" Billy states, believing the Count to be merely the product of the movies in a nice pre-*Scream* piece of post-modernism. However, just as the Dracula of Hammer claimed his first male victim in the form of Johnny Alucard that year, so the two boys become Mamuwalde's first victims as they prise open the coffin only to reveal his more hirsute vampiric form as Blacula, free from his coffin confines.

The tone shifts immediately, is more brutal and sharper after the limp-wristed shenanigans between the pair, helped by the ferocity of Marshall's performance after the richly aristocratic turn we saw in the pre-credits sequence. With him in tow, any potential sniggering at the rather bushy outcrops from his cheeks and the widow's peak of his afro are soon dissipated.

I really like *Blacula* a lot, and it is fair to say Marshall holds the whole scenario together with his impressive presence. There are some exciting moments such as a horde of vampires being repelled with oil lamps and subsequently writhing around in flames, and just to see and hear the contemporary milieu and Black characters in this tale of vampirism marks the picture out as something special far beyond the *Count Yorga* features.

There is an atmospheric moment resonant of more gothic times when Thalmus Rasulala's Dr Gordon Thomas - of the Scientific Investigation Division of LAPD - digs the grave of Billy whom he suspects of having been turned into a vampire. Watched on by his partner Michelle, played with grace by Denise Nicholas, both are given the fright of their lives as Billy leaps out of his coffin before Thomas manages to slam a stake through his heart with his spade with two hard thrusts. It's a decent jump scare,

I must admit.

Vonetta McGee plays both Luva and Michelle's sister Tina. Her Blaxploitation credits that same year were *Hammer* and *Melinda*, with *Shaft in Africa* following in 1973. She gives the part of Tina heartfelt empathy; in lesser hands it may not have come across quite so believably how she succumbs to Mamuwalde's charms, his story of how he became a vampire, and her love for him in a relatively short space of time. I buy it totally thanks to her sensitive portrayal.

One niggle that does bother me - whilst sat with Tina, Michelle and Thomas, a woman named Nancy takes their photograph for Michelle's birthday, but Mamuwalde shields himself and then later as Blacula tears into her home, bites her, and crushes the developed photo that does not bear his figure. So how does a prince from 1780 know that a vampire casts no image, let alone know about photography in the first place? This is where Torres and Koenig's lack of experience as horror scribes comes into focus - they've inserted this piece of business there because that is the lore, no matter the lack of narrative context.

There is some knowing humour in place, as Mamuwalde orders a Bloody Mary at the nightclub, and the morgue attendant Sam casually scratches his hair with his steel hook of an arm. We do, however, have two uses of the 'n' word. On both occasions they are spoken by and to black people, having been written by two Caucasian writers who also use the word faggot, and not by either Bobby or

Billy. Great intentions in the script could really have done without these, even in America in the early '70s and the ubiquitousness of the slurs.

Blacula does have some decent complexities of character in its favour, with the viewer invited to feel sympathy for Mamuwalde even in the face of all the deaths incurred by his vampiric thirst and wrath. He also seems to have a dual personality at play, for whilst he is urbane and well-mannered as Mamuwalde, he snarls and barks with that tremendously deep, booming voice as his Blacula side comes to the fore.

Voluntarily walking out into direct sunlight gives the character final dignity, despite the maggots crawling from his decomposing, boiling head, but with box office receipts nudging over $1 million against its $500,000 budget, Blacula wouldn't rest in pieces for long…

Mother Loa has died without naming her voodoo-practising successor. Brash, arrogant Willis demands he be the new head of the cult, even though they favour the more sensitive Lisa. In revenge, he seeks out a voodoo priest, who hands him the bones of Blacula!

These he places within a circle of candles on bricks, and as a storm brews, he wrings the neck of a blue-smeared dove before slitting its neck and pouring blood into a bowl, as he chants an invocation. This is the effective and atmospheric prologue to *Scream Blacula Scream* as the revived Prince of Shadows is revived, only to curse his resurrector in return.

With director Bob Kelljan of the *Count Yorga* movies in tow (presumably not angry about that crate shot being re-used in *Blacula*!), returning scriptwriters Torres and Koenig - along with contributor Maurice Jules - invest this sequel with a decent combination of evocative horror and knowing humour. Dressed to kill, as it were, Willis is dismayed to find he casts no reflection in the mirror: "Look, man, I don't mind being a vampire and all that shit,

but this really ain't hip!"

William Marshall once more dons the cape, this time red-lined, and brings the usual commanding and dignified air to Mamuwalde, coming across animalistic and snarling as Blacula. Only this time he is on a personal mission to free himself of the curse of vampirism, and to do so he needs the help of Lisa and her voodoo skills. Pam Grier brings the part a fragility mixed with her inherited gift that fleshes out the part well. In the same year this follow-up

was released, she starred as the titular *Coffy* and went on to be one of the most strident performers in cinema, her cult status earning her adulation by Quentin Tarantino and the role of *Jackie Brown* in 1997.

Famous for his role as Sergeant Phil Esterhaus in *Hill Street Blues*, Michael Conrad here is Lieutenant Harley Dunlop, the cynical foil to Don Mitchell's Justin Carter, a former officer and collector of African items of antiquary, including Mamuwalde's bride Luva's necklace! He soon comes to suspect the gracious former African prince, and during a wonderfully tense scene over a glass of red wine - the hue of which he teases as resembling blood - Justin goads Mamuwalde with 'ridiculous' talk of Count Dracula actually being real, according to the books he's read. The tension positively simmers.

Elsewhere, Willis is slowly forming a cult of his own, as the house he is looking after is slowly filling with vampires who are forbidden by Blacula to harm Lisa. The same feeling of a spreading geometry of vampires is felt here; you bite one, they bite two, etc, and the gothic background to their kind is nicely counterpointed by the contemporary Los Angeles setting. Much as I love *Dracula*

A.D. 1972, these two *Blacula* movies really show how to combine the two elements to their fullest potential.

This modernity is showcased by a scene in which Mamuwalde strolls past a variety of sex shops and peep shows, expressing distaste along the way and even refusing the attention of a lady of the night. Her pimps don't take too kindly to this and demand he hand over his money. To this, Mamuwalde retorts angrily: "You've made a slave of your sister. You're still slaves, imitating your slave masters!" A rather fine piece of political commentary, before Blacula lashes out and kills the pair, having already killed Lisa's friend Gloria.

Trying to convince the dogged Harley there is a vampire loose in the city is no easy task for Justin. The Lieutenant already professed no sympathies to black people, especially those who practice voodoo, and as far as he's concerned, bodies with two bite marks on their necks can only mean snakes, as well as the fact that "…you guys drink blood," as he says alarmingly at one point.

Rather neatly, a police photographer shows Harley and Justin images of the recent scene of crime. There are the ambulance men right enough, but where there should be

chants over his voodoo doll. Kelljan is on fine form with these intermingled scenes, leaving us breathlessly hoping the police don't barge in on Lisa and Mamuwalde before the ritual is completed.

Spoiler alert - Justin does indeed express remarkable bad timing, leaving Blacula to rear up and attack, leaving Lisa aghast at his bloodthirsty rage. With a spare arrow from a crossbow, she lets rip with the voodoo doll, closing the film on a sudden overhead shot and freeze-frame as Blacula screams out, fading out on a rather lovely song that leaves us full of sympathy for the once great African prince.

Building on the *Yorga* films, and indeed the previous decade's *Rosemary's Baby* and *Night of the Living Dead* in terms of present-day set horrors, as well as riding the crest of the Blaxploitation craze, the *Blacula* duo present us with a protagonist/antagonist we really root for, as well as bringing out the horror he leaves in his wake. The largely black cast of characters are portrayed roundly and offer audiences a glimpse into a world a lot of whom would have been unfamiliar with, so no bad thing there. And the knowing humour makes sure there are no unintentional slips into the ridiculous. The whole presentation jives along just fine.

a body in their arms is nothing at all. Again, vampire lore and the modern day meet very effectively.

There is also a nod to *Yorga* when Justin insists Harley's men be armed with stakes before they storm the house at which Blacula resides, each man handed a piece of sharpened garden fence!

The scenes between Marshall and Grier work extremely well as Lisa accepts Mamuwalde's story of how he came to be cursed in the first place. She had already felt a connection to him during his revival, as a crack in the fire she had been gazing at juxtaposed to the eruption in flames of his bones during Willis' summoning. There is no romance here as with Tina, more a deep held respect for each other.

The voodoo scenes are pretty much of the standard movie type, so only demonstrate a crude, simplified and audience-friendly variety, much as Roger Moore's debut James Bond film *Live and Let Die* was doing the same year. They even have an actor in common with Arnold Williams showcasing his magnificent sideburns as the cab driver who kidnaps Bond, and a friend of Willis' in *Scream Blacula Scream*.

The ritual still makes for an engaging climax as we cut from Lisa's attempts to rid Mamuwalde of his Blacula persona at the same time the police storm the house. As vampires bite, and officers stake, Mamuwalde writhes in pain as Lisa

Time after TIMEAA

by Peter Sawford

Over the years, Jack the Ripper has been well served by filmmakers. He was the inspiration for Ivor Novello's character in Alfred Hitchcock's *The Lodger* (1926), he was an avenging doctor in 1959's *Jack the Ripper*, he was chased twice by Sherlock Holmes in *A Study in Terror* (1965) and the excellent *Murder by Decree* (1979) and, more recently, was named and shamed in the slightly iffy *From Hell* (2001). But in 1979, *Time After Time* took a different approach to the story and sent Jack to another time and place to continue his deadly killing spree.

A film about Jack the Ripper wouldn't be a film about Jack the Ripper if it didn't open on a foggy night in old Victorian London, and *Time After Time* doesn't disappoint. An unfortunate young lady of the night, in the wrong place at the wrong time, meets a smooth-talking, well-dressed gentleman and is so enamoured by the tune his pocket watch plays that her expression barely has a chance to change as his knife slowly, but definitely not silently, slices her open. The Ripper leaves the scene, but when the victim is found quicker than expected, the police are able to give chase while the trail (and indeed the body) are still warm.

At his home, H.G. Wells (Malcolm McDowell) is entertaining friends at a dinner party with his ideas and visions for the future and the utopian society he envisages everyone living in. He refuses to tell them his big secret until the last guest, Dr. John Stevenson (David Warner), arrives. Once Stevenson shows up, Wells takes his guests to his basement and reveals, much to their collective amusement, his fully functioning (at least in theory) time

machine complete with non-return key and vaporising equalizer.

The evening is interrupted when the police arrive and announce they've tracked Jack the Ripper to the address. A quick search of the house reveals that Dr. Stevenson's bag contains bloody gloves. Unsurprisingly, the good Doctor has vanished while the search is taking place.

Once the police and his guests have left, Wells guesses Stevenson must have used the time machine to escape. He rushes to the basement just as the machine reappears due to Wells having the non-return key. Wells quickly follows Stevenson into the future and finds himself in 1979 San Francisco with its traffic, air travel, telephones, fast food outlets and a dozen other things that confuse and bewilder him.

When Wells first arrives in 1979, he finds himself at a museum hosting an exhibition dedicated to himself! This allows him to change his glasses which got broken during the journey with a pair he kept in the bureau which had been in his study back in 1893.

While searching for Stevenson, Wells realises that his quarry will need money, so trawls around the dozens of banks in the city. In doing so, he meets Amy Robbins (Mary Steenburgen), an employee at the Chartered Bank of London. She finds herself immediately attracted to him and decides to show him the city. As their relationship grows, Wells continues to try to stop Stevenson. He must somehow convince a less-than-interested San Francisco Police Department about Stevenson's intentions, and find a way of telling Robbins who he really is and where he's

really from without her thinking he's completely mad.

It doesn't take long for Wells to realise that the future he's found himself in doesn't square with the vision he'd talked about so often with his friends. World Wars, street violence and the general apathy people show in their everyday feelings, problems and fears confound him. To Wells, the world has simply sunk deeper into an abyss.

His disappointment with the future slowly wears him down, his frustration at his apparent inability to stop Stevenson eats him up inside, and you feel it's only his guilty conscience at having released a monster onto this future world that stops him from jumping back into the machine and heading back to Victorian times.

The one ray of light in this strange, unfamiliar and disappointing world is Amy. Strong-willed, independent, sexually free-minded and bursting with personality, Amy is everything Wells ever wanted from a woman and he can hardly believe he's had to travel halfway round the world and 75+ years into the future to meet the woman of his dreams. Smitten from almost the first moment he meets her, Wells' despair at the danger Amy is in while he's being held at the police station is palpable. His desolation at being informed a body has been found at her home, and the thought of having lost the woman who could be his one true love, is profound.

McDowell was, for many years, a favourite of independent filmmakers with a certain cynical and idiosyncratic view of life such as Lindsay Anderson and Stanley Kubrick. Some of his greatest roles include *If. .. .* (1968), *A Clockwork Orange* (1971) and *O Lucky Man!* (1973) which McDowell also cowrote. Before starting work on *Time After Time*, he'd just completed filming Tinto Brass' controversial *Caligula* and wanted something as far from the sex and violence of that notorious film as possible. McDowell gives Wells a vulnerability in all his encounters with Stevenson, but a certain degree of confidence and an almost insatiable thirst for knowledge. He portrays Wells as brave and resourceful, but deep down knows that his friend was, and always will be, one step ahead when it comes to positioning his pieces skilfully on the chessboard of life.

Steenburgen was discovered by Jack Nicholson, who'd cast her as the female lead in *Goin' South* (1978) which he was directing as well as starring in, but you would never guess *Time After Time* was only her second screen outing. You get the feeling that a fair bit of Steenburgen's own feisty personality sneaks into her performance as she actively chases and charms this curious Englishman who's walked into her bank. Her quiet acceptance of her apparent fate is in marked contrast to her anger when Wells finally tells her the truth about why he's there and how he got there. The voice may be quiet, the demeanour calm, but there's a raging fire not far below her surface.

While Wells is disappointed and appalled by the world he's travelled to, John Stevenson feels totally at home in

these new anarchic surroundings. Cold, calculating, self-absorbed, nihilistic and completely amoral, Stevenson is, as he says, entirely at home and by the murderous standards of the day, even considered somewhat of an amateur (though I doubt his many victims share his somewhat modest opinion of his talents). Stevenson's charm and good looks allow him to select his prey whenever the urge to kill is strong, and his total lack of emotion makes him able to kill even the sweetest victim with no more thought than he'd give to swatting a fly. Stevenson is always one step ahead of Wells and constantly out-thinking him as easily as he did on the chessboard back in 1893 in an earlier scene. That said, his acceptance of his fate at the end shows that even he knows he has to be stopped as he lacks the emotional strength or desire to stop himself.

Warner had developed a reputation as an excellent character-actor who could effortlessly steal scenes. Like McDowell, he'd worked with some great directors, such as Sam Peckinpah on three occasions (the motor cycle-riding preacher in *The Ballad of Cable Hogue*, the slow witted Henry Niles in *Straw Dogs*, and a cynical German soldier in *Cross of Iron*). He'd famously been decapitated in Richard Donner's *The Omen* (1976) and played the duplicitous Sir Edmund Appleton in *The Thirty-Nine Steps* (1978), the first of many evil antagonist roles he would be offered over the years. From the first scene, we're never in doubt of Warner's evil presence. Although masked when he dispatches his first victim, his voice - so unmistakeable, so velvet smooth - is heard saying sweet nothings to his next target. Throughout the film, Warner has a stillness about him that adds to Stevenson's sinister demeanour, a

classic case of less is more, as he lulls his quarry into his web.

The main cast is nicely rounded out by Charles Cioffi as the disbelieving police lieutenant whose patronising attitude when Wells initially visits quickly changes to a more robust approach when he realises he's close to cornering a serial killer.

The film was based on an uncompleted (at the time) story by Karl Alexander and was quickly optioned by screenwriter Nicholas Meyer after reading the few completed pages. Meyer had previously written 'The Seven-Per-Cent Solution' (1975) after co-writing *Invasion of the Bee Girls* two years before with Sylvia Schneble. He bought *Time After Time* with the view of stepping into the director's chair himself for the first time. Perhaps understandably, given that it's his first directorial attempt, Meyer directs in a nice, uncomplicated, unfussy manner allowing the story to unravel at its own pace while adding some nice touches to the story, particularly as he contrasts Wells' Victorian sensibilities with Amy's more modern and aggressive attitude towards sex.

The wonderful score was one of the last ever composed by Hollywood great Miklos Rozsa and includes a leitmotif (perhaps dark motif might be more appropriate) whenever Stevenson appears. Rozsa also utilises the trick so brilliantly used by Ennio Morricone in *For a Few Dollars More* (1965) and, to a lesser extent, *The Good, the Bad and the Ugly* (1966), of a tune being played on a gentleman's pocket-watch to signify either an impending death or Stevenson's malevolent presence. Such is the timeless elegance of Rozsa's score it could almost be picked up and put in any film noir from the '40s and not sound a note out of place. Even the opening titles hark back nicely to the films of the '40s, with the titles playing over a simple background to the dramatic, ominous chords of his main theme.

Rozsa would win a Saturn Award for the score along with Nicholas Meyer (Best Writing) and Mary Steenburgen (Best Actress). McDowell and Warner would pick up acting nominations, and Meyer was in the running for

Best Director, while Sal Anthony and Yvonne Kubis were nominated for Best Costumes.

One area *Time After Time* was unlikely to be nominated (indeed, the one aspect which dates it somewhat) is the special effects of the time machine. The initial moments of the flight are crude to say the least and could have been taken from any number of late '60s/early '70s Gerry Anderson TV shows. It looks cheap and probably was. Meyer evidently realised this and changed it for a simple recording of various historical events to mark the passing of time. *The Time Machine*, made nearly twenty years earlier, made a much better job of depicting its machine travelling through the millennia but it's a small quibble in an otherwise superb film.

The film premiered at the Toronto International Film Festival on 7th September 1979 and received mostly positive reviews from the critics, though Meyer's direction came in for some criticism. It was the inspiration for the 1984 Cyndi Lauper song of the same name, a song Lauper started writing after seeing the film title in a TV guide. It also spawned a 2016 television series which broadly followed the same storyline but had Wells following Stevenson to New York in 2017. The series starred Freddie Stroma as Wells, Josh Bowman as John Stevenson (aka Jack the Ripper), Genesis Rodriguez as Jane Walker and Vanessa Anders as Wells' great-great-granddaughter. The Amy Robbins character was written out completely. Twelve episodes were filmed (each episode titled after a phrase from the Cyndi Lauper song), but it was unceremoniously dropped from the broadcasting schedules after five had aired. The full twelve were shown in a handful of countries outside the United States.

For many years, the 1979 version of *Time After Time* disappeared from TV schedules, but later it developed something of a cult following with several critics lauding it as a minor classic.

Some films just prove that if they're well written, well-acted, simply directed and tell a good story, then huge star names and a budget of millions aren't needed. They're just great films which can be watched… well, time after time.

CLOSING CREDITS

James Aaron
James is an American writer and film lover living in Kentucky with his wife and two dogs. He is the author (as Aaron Saylor) of three novels, including 'Sewerville' and 'Adventures in Terror', the latter of which is set during the horror movie and video store boom of the 1980s.

Simon J. Ballard
Simon lives in Oxford and works in a Saxon Tower. He regularly contributes to the magazines 'We Belong Dead' (and its various book releases), 'The Dark Side', 'Infinity', 'Cinema of the '70s/'80s' and 'Scream'. He has written a short story collection, 'Edgelands of Fear', with Hammer music expert David Huckvale. His first published work was a Top Tip in 'Viz' of which he is justifiably proud, and he once read 'The Black Cat' to a group of goths at his regular LGBTQI+ pub The Jolly Farmers. He is currently working on a book with filmmaker David Wickes.

Rachel Bellwoar
Rachel is a writer for 'Comicon', 'Diabolique' magazine and 'Flickering Myth'. If she could have any director fim a biopic about her life it would be Aki Kaurismäki.

David Michael Brown
David is a British ex-pat living in Sydney. Working as a freelance writer he has contributed to 'The Big Issue', 'TV Week', 'GQ', 'Rolling Stone' and 'Empire Magazine Australia', where he was Senior Editor for almost eight years. He is presently writing a book on the film music of German electronic music pioneers Tangerine Dream and researching the work of Andy Warhol associate and indie filmmaker Paul Morrissey for a forthcoming project.

Jonathon Dabell
Jonathon was born in Nottingham in 1976. He is a huge film fan and considers '70s cinema his favourite decade. He has written for 'Cinema Retro' and 'We Belong Dead', and co-authored 'More Than a Psycho: The Complete Films of Anthony Perkins' and 'Ultimate Warrior: The Complete Films of Yul Brynner' with his wife. He lives in Yorkshire with his wife, three kids, three cats and two rabbits!

David Flack
David was born and bred in Cambridge. He has had reviews published in 'We Belong Dead' and 'Cinema of the '80s'. He loves watching, talking, reading and writing about film and participating on film forums. The best film he has seen in over 55 years of watching is *Jaws* (1975). The worst is *The Creeping Terror* (1963) or anything by Andy Milligan.

Brian Gregory
Brian is an English tutor who both reviews and makes films in his spare time. He has his first horror feature film currently in post-production. He has written several articles for 'We Belong Dead'. Originally from North Harrow, Brian now resides in Hove, Sussex. Among his favourite '70s films would be: *High Plains Drifter*, *Scum*, *Annie Hall*, *Phase IV* and *The Tenant*. His website is www.gregoryfilms.co.uk

John Harrison
John is a Melbourne, Australia-based freelance writer and film historian who has written for numerous genre publications, including 'Fatal Visions', 'Cult Movies', 'Is It Uncut?', 'Monster!' and 'Weng's Chop'. Harrison is also the author of the Headpress book 'Hip Pocket Sleaze: The Lurid World of Vintage Adult Paperbacks', has recorded audio commentaries for Kino Lorber, and composed the booklet essays for the Australian Blu-ray releases of *Thirst*, *Dead Kids* and *The Survivor*. 'Wildcat!', Harrison's book on the film and television career of former child evangelist Marjoe Gortner, was published by Bear Manor in 2020.

James Lecky
James is an actor, writer and occasional stand-up comedian who has had a lifelong obsession with cinema, beginning with his first visit to the Palace Cinema in Derry (now long since gone) to see *Chitty Chitty Bang Bang* when he was six. Since then, he has happily wallowed in cinema of all kinds but has a particular fondness for Hammer movies, spaghetti westerns, Euro-crime and samurai films.

Bryan C. Kuriawa
Based in New Jersey, Bryan has spent many years diving into the world of movies. Introduced to the Three Stooges by his grandfather and Japanese cinema when he was eight, he's wandered on his own path, ignoring popular opinions. Willing to discuss and defend everything from Jesus Franco's surreal outings to the 007 masterpiece *Moonraker*, nothing is off-limits. Some of his favorite filmmakers include Ishiro Honda, Jacques Tati, Lewis Gilbert, Jesus Franco and Jun Fukuda.

Tom Lisanti
Tom is an award-winning author specializing in writing about 1960s/1970s Hollywood. His most recent book (#10) is 'Carol Lynley: Her Film & TV Career in Thrillers, Fantasy & Suspense' from BearManor Media. He also has written recent magazine articles for 'Films of the Golden Age' and 'Cinema Retro'. His newest books due in 2023 are 'Dueling Harlows: Race to the Silver Screen Expanded Ed.' and 'Ryan's Hope: An Oral History of Daytime's Ground-Breaking Soap' from Kensington Books. Tom posts regularly on Facebook, Twitter, and his website, sixtiescinema.com. He resides in New York.

Stephen Mosley

Stephen is an actor and writer, whose books include 'Christopher Lee: The Loneliness of Evil' (Midnight Marquee Press), 'Klawseye: The Imagination Snatcher of Phantom Island', 'The Lives & Deaths of Morbius Mozella', 'TOWN' and 'The Boy Who Loved Simone Simon'. His film articles have appeared in such magazines as 'Midnight Marquee', 'We Belong Dead' and 'The Dark Side'. His film credits include the evil Ear Goblin in *Kenneth*; the eponymous paranormal investigator of *Kestrel Investigates*; the shady farmer, James, in *Contradiction*; and a blink-and-you'll-miss-it appearance opposite Sam Neill in *Peaky Blinders*. Stephen is one half of the music duo Collinson Twin and lives in a dungeon near Leeds.

Kevin Nickelson

Kevin has been a fan of cinema of all genres and decades since age 4. As he grew older he found his passions for dissecting various aspects of film and decided to marry this obsession with his ability for creative writing into writing about film. Kevin has written for 'Scarlet the Magazine', the 'Van Helsing Confidential' and the site classic-horror.com. Currently, he writes for 'We Belong Dead' magazine and books, 'Scary Monsters' magazine, horrornews. net and will soon be working for 'Scream' magazine. Kevin is also co-host of the Grim and Bloody podcast produced by Death's Parade Film Fest.

Allen Rubinstein

Allen grew up in an upper-middle-class neighborhood in suburban Connecticut. He writes about movies and history and tries to reveal the truth wherever possible. He works with his wife on a teaching organization called The Poetry Salon (www. thepoetrysalon.com) in Costa Rica while taking care of far too many cats. He has not yet told his parents that he's an anarcho-syndicalist.

Peter Sawford

Peter was born in Essex in 1964 so considers himself a child of the '70s. A self-confessed film buff, he loves watching, reading about and talking about cinema. A frustrated writer his whole life, he's only recently started submitting what he writes to magazines. His favourite director is Alfred Hitchcock with Billy Wilder running him a close second. He still lives in Essex with his wife and works as an IT trainer and when not watching films he's normally panicking over who West Ham are playing next.

Aaron Stielstra

Aaron was born in Ann Arbor, Michigan and grew up in Tucson, AZ. and NYC. He is an actor, writer, illustrator, soundtrack composer and director. After moving to Italy in 2012, he has appeared in 4 spaghetti westerns and numerous horror-thrillers - all of them unnecessarily wet. He recently directed the punk rock comedy *Excretion: the Shocking True Story of the Football Moms*. His favorite '70s actor is Joe Spinell.

Ian Talbot Taylor

After early short story successes, Ian began editing music fanzines and spent decades acting, directing and adjudicating in amateur theatre for the Greater Manchester Drama Federation. He writes for 'The Dark Side', 'Infinity', 'Scream', 'Fantastic Fifties', 'Halls of Horror' and 'We Belong Dead' (and is on the editorial team of the latter). His book on the films of Jenny Agutter appeared in 2021. Ian has progressed from 'prose dabbler' to prolific fiction writer, contributing to and co-editing the BHF Books of Horror. He recently released the collaborative fiction collection 'Spoken in Whispers' and also presents shows for Radio M29 .

Dr. Andrew C. Webber

Dr. W. has been a Film, Media and English teacher and examiner for over 35 years and his passion for the cinema remains undiminished all these years later. As far as he is concerned, a platform is where you wait for the 08.16 to Victoria; dropping is something that louts do with litter; and streaming is how you might feel if you were in *Night of the Hunter* being hotly pursued by Robert Mitchum with "Hate" tattooed on his knuckles and Stanley Cortez doing the cinematography.

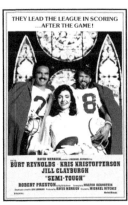